ONE IN THE SPIRIT

ONE IN THE SPIRIT

DAVID WATSON

Hodder & Stoughton

LONDON SYDNEY AUCKLAND

British Library Cataloguing in Publication Data
A record for this book is available from the British Library

ISBN 0 340 71392 5

Printed and bound in Great Britain by
Clays Ltd, St Ives plc

Hodder and Stoughton Ltd
A Division of Hodder Headline PLC
338 Euston Road
London NW1 3BH

ACKNOWLEDGMENTS

THE material in this book stems largely from the addresses given by the author at the Annual Conference of the Colleges of Education Christian Unions, at Swanwick in April 1972.

The author acknowledges gratefully some ideas for his third and fifth chapters from the commentary on 1 Corinthians 12–14 by Arnold Bittlinger, *Gifts and Graces*, published by Hodder and Stoughton.

He is also very grateful to John Freeth and to the Publications Committee of the Inter-Varsity Press for their helpful comments on reading the initial manuscript, and to Mrs. Joan Johnson and Miss Frances Smith for their typing.

Biblical quotations unless otherwise stated are from the Revised Standard Version.

CONTENTS

PREFACE

No small paperback can begin to convey the glorious complexity of the work of the Holy Spirit of God. The selection of the material in this book has been guided by two factors.

In the first place, these chapters are substantially the main addresses at one annual conference, and were never originally intended for wider publication. And in one short conference on the person and work of the Spirit, what has *not* been said may sadly be more conspicuous than what *has* been said. Undoubtedly, the Holy Spirit is at work in a multitude of quiet and unspectacular ways in the Church as a whole, not least in the steady worship and witness of churches and fellowships of all sizes which are to be found all over the world. Wherever Christians are seeking to honour God, in their prayer and study of the Scriptures, in their public and private witness, in their preaching and teaching of the word of God, and in their love and compassion towards those in need, you can expect to see evidence of the Spirit's activity. No one group within the true Church of God has a monopoly of the Spirit's presence.

In the second place, I have deliberately aimed the material at some of the points of 'hot debate' at the present time—notably the charismatic movement, which opens up questions about the baptism and fullness of the Spirit, the gifts of the Spirit, guidance, praise and the whole question of Christian experience.

As much of my present work is in connection with evangelistic missions, mainly in universities but also in churches, it is a matter of great personal concern and sadness to see Christians divided over the work of the Spirit, when undoubtedly it is his intention to make us united. It seems to many of us that, with the growing spiritual hunger of today, opportunities for proclaiming Christ in the power of the Spirit abound on every side. However, above everything else we need to be united in love—'one in the Spirit, one in the Lord'. My simple prayer in writing this book is that God may graciously use it, in a measure known only to him, to draw Christians together with a new desire to love one another as we love him, in obedience to Christ's command. I am not expecting for a moment that everyone will agree with what I have said. But as Paul exhorted the Christians at Ephesus, may God make us into one united body, 'with all lowliness and meekness, with patience, forbearing one another in love, eager to maintain the unity of the Spirit in the bond of peace'.

CHAPTER I

THE PERSON OF THE HOLY SPIRIT

In recent years the most lively debate within the Church has centred round the person and work of the Holy Spirit. Many are testifying to spiritual renewal in their lives; others are complaining of dissensions and divisions in their churches. Theological controversy rages round the 'gifts of the Spirit' and the 'baptism of the Spirit'. The amazing development of the 'charismatic movement' has thrilled some, angered others and puzzled still more. At least there is a general agreement that a rediscovery of the life and power of the Spirit is one of the greatest needs of our day. Indeed, Dr. Carl Bates once made the remark that 'if God were to take the Holy Spirit out of our midst today, about ninety-five per cent of what we are doing in our churches would go on, and we would not know the difference.' For many years the Holy Spirit has been 'the Displaced Person of the Trinity'.

Yet, undoubtedly, the Spirit of God was the key to everything in the New Testament Church. The fifth book of the New Testament should really be called the Acts of the Holy Spirit. If God had taken the Holy Spirit out of their midst in those days, about ninety-five per cent of what they were doing in their churches would have ceased immediately. Everyone would have known the difference.

There are a number of striking trends in the world today which are of particular significance in view of our past neglect of the Holy Spirit.

First, there is an obvious impatience with the organised Church. There is an uncomfortable truth in this parody of a famous hymn:

> *Like a mighty tortoise*
> *Moves the Church of God;*
> *Brothers we are treading*
> *Where we've always trod;*
> *We are all divided,*
> *Many bodies we,*
> *Very strong on doctrine,*
> *Weak on charity.*

Constantly, I find that the number one obstacle to personal faith in Christ is 'the Church'. So much of its activities seem out-of-touch and unreal. What is the answer to the huge irrelevance of the Church? What do you do when its articles of faith do not ring a bell in your personal experience? There are two obvious answers, and both are happening today at the same time. Either you change your theology to fit your experience, and say that 'God is dead' (a convenient slogan for many today, whose *experience* of God is dead, for one reason or another). Or, keeping your Biblical theology, you can thirst for the living God until you have a true, deep, personal experience through the power of the Holy Spirit. 'My soul thirsts for God, for the living God. When shall I come and behold the face of God? My tears have been my food day and night, while men say to me continually, "Where is your God?" ' (Psalm 42 : 2–3). Is not that precisely what the world is saying to the Church today : 'Where is your God?' Where indeed?

Secondly, there is a feverish activity to reorganise the Church. An article in the *New York Times* recently made this coment : 'When an institution no longer knows what it is doing, it starts trying to do everything.' Many Christians today are weary of reports, reforms and reunion schemes, discussions, dialogues and debates. We spend our time talking to ourselves while the world plunges headlong into suicide and despair. And it is in this context that the primary need for a dynamic spiritual renewal by the Holy Spirit of God becomes obvious and urgent. We lack the fire and passion which has always been the mark of the Spirit's presence. Take for example the case of John Wesley :

'John Wesley had a strangely warmed heart allied to a strangely cool head. The latter, on its own, will always find deeply convincing reasons for playing it safe, remaining open-ended, instituting a dialogue, exploring in depth, setting up a commission, running a pilot scheme, circulating a paper, doing some research—in fact anything rather than go out on to the streets of Jerusalem drunk with the Spirit, and showing others how.'[1]

Thirdly, there is an alarming rise in occultism, East-

[1] 'Marksman' in *British Weekly*, quoted in *And there was Light*, by John Capon, Lutterworth, p. 115.

ern mysticism, and the whole drug culture. Ouija boards are sold as toys. Séances and various forms of spiritism abound. The Church of England has recently stressed the need for trained exorcists to deal effectively with enormous pastoral problems resulting from psychic disturbances. No longer can such phenomena be regarded as a recrudescence of medieval superstition. For any sceptic the reality of occult powers has been amply demonstrated by the careful researches of Dr. Kurt E. Koch in such books as *Christian Counselling and Occultism, Between Christ and Satan, Occult Bondage and Deliverance* and *The Devil's Alphabet.*

I was speaking at Magee University, Londonderry, one evening, on the Person of Jesus Christ. Two students came up to talk to me at the end of the meeting. 'We went to a séance for the first time last night,' said one of them, 'and we were astonished by the reality of it all and by the accuracy of answers given to various questions that were asked.' I explained that not only is spiritism expressly and repeatedly condemned in Scripture,[2] but in nine cases out of ten those dabbling in such forbidden practices are harmed physically, mentally or spiritually (Dr. Koch's conclusion). However, my two friends were not so easily dissuaded. 'We've been to masses of religious meetings; and always it's been words, words, words, words. Now at least we have found *spiritual reality.*'

Everywhere there is this profound spiritual hunger, a search for some kind of spiritual reality. 'My soul thirsts for God, for the living God'—for something

[2] Deuteronomy 18: 9ff.; Leviticus 19: 26, 31; 20: 6, 27; 1 Chronicles 10: 13–14; Isaiah 8: 19–20; Acts 19: 19; Galatians 5: 20; Revelation 21: 8; 22: 15 *et al.*

that is real, in terms of personal experience. 'It is ironical,' said Kenneth Leech, 'that at a time when Christians are feverishly running about sorting out reunion schemes and administrative reorganisations, and young clergy are desperately trying to be "with it", the whole psychedelic scene is turning to oriental mystics for a spirituality which it has assumed Western Christianity is too superficial to provide.'

Fourthly, there has been a remarkable growth of Pentecostalism, not only in the recognised Pentecostal denomination, which has exploded at an extraordinary rate in seventy years, but more recently in all the traditional churches all over the world.

Now, whatever our views might be about the theology of such experience, what is the reason for this astonishing phenomenon? Let me suggest at least a part of the explanation.

For centuries the Holy Spirit has been effectively subordinated, either to the Bible (by Protestants) or to the Church (by Roman Catholics). In his book *Baptism in the Holy Spirit*, Dr. James Dunn makes this perceptive comment. He is talking about the three main streams of Christianity: Catholics, Protestants and Pentecostals. With the Catholics, he writes,

the Spirit became more and more confined to 'the Church', until in all but name 'the Church' stood above the Spirit. To all intents and purposes the Spirit became the property of the Church, with the gift of the Spirit tied to and determined by a ritual act, and authority to bestow the Spirit confined to the bishop ... Against this extreme sacramentalism and sacerdotalism Protestants reacted, and in their reaction the emphasis was shifted from water-baptism to preaching and personal faith, with authority centred in the Bible rather than in the Church ... The Spirit, however, did not return to prominence, largely owing to Protestant suspicion and hatred of the Anabaptists. He was the begetter of faith and of all good, and the reality of his manifestations in the apostolic age was accepted, but little was said about the gift of the Spirit as such, and the charismata were thought to have ceased with the apostles. In scholastic Protestantism the Spirit became in effect subordinate to the Bible ... Where Catholics fastened on to the objectivity of the sacraments, Protestants fastened on to the objectivity of the Bible ... Like earlier 'enthusiasts' Pentecostals have reacted against both these extremes. Against the mechanical sacramentalism of extreme Catholicism and the dead biblicist orthodoxy of extreme Protestantism they have shifted the focus of attention to the *experience* of the Spirit. That the Spirit, and particularly the gift of the Spirit, was a *fact of experience* in the lives of the earliest Christians has been too obvious to require elaboration.[3]

Dorothy Sayers once expressed it pithily like this: 'There are those who would worship the Father, the Son and the Virgin Mary; those who believe in the Father, the Son and the Holy Scriptures; those who found their faith on the Father, the Son and the Church; and there are even those who seem to derive their spiritual power from the Father, the Son and

[3] op. cit., S.C.M., pp. 224ff.

the minister!' The Pentecostal explosion has largely been a reaction to this, with a fresh recognition of the Third Person of the Trinity, and a deep longing for the same wind of the Spirit that energised believers both in the first century and in all the revivals of the Church down the years.

THE SPIRIT AS A PERSON

Let me stress from the start that we are looking primarily at a person, not primarily at a doctrine. Of course, God has revealed himself in his word, and a right understanding of his word, in the form of doctrinal statements, is of the utmost importance. Nevertheless, the way we approach a proposition and the way we approach a person are two very different things, especially when that person is God. Indeed, I believe that part of the controversy about the Holy Spirit today stems from the fact that, in our weakness and foolishness, we try to tie up the Spirit with a set of neat doctrinal phrases. Therefore, we fight over words of secondary importance, such as 'baptism' and 'fullness', because we want to get the Holy Spirit 'taped'. But the Third Person of the Godhead will never be taped by finite humanity. It is like trying to bottle the wind; as soon as you have got it, you have lost it!

By this, I am not implying for one moment that a right understanding of such doctrinal phrases is of no importance. Far from it! But splits and divisions in the Church have frequently been caused by Christians fighting over secondary matters, when all along we should humbly acknowledge our spiritual poverty and unitedly seek for a greater realisation of the living God in our midst. Dr. Billy Graham has put it like this:

I wonder if one of the secrets of pentecostalism cannot be learned by our main-stream churches with the great emphasis upon the Holy Spirit. The time has come to give the Holy Spirit his rightful place. We need to learn what it means to be baptised with the Holy Spirit, we need to know what Paul meant when he wrote, 'Be filled with the Spirit'. Give it any terminology you like, we need to accept it, to get something, for we do not have the same dynamic that the early church had. The Bible teaches that the Holy Spirit is like the wind, and who can tell the wind what to do? Another symbol is the dove, and who can tell a dove when it can fly into the sky and what way to go? Water—living water, that shall be poured out in a mighty torrent—all these symbols express the sovereignty of God. We dig our little trenches and we say, 'O God, you are going to work this way, and only this way.' But God breaks out and does it in his own way.

SYMBOLS OF THE HOLY SPIRIT

Most Christians find no great problem in thinking about God the Father or God the Son. But the imagination finds it much harder to picture God the Spirit. In part, this may be due to the fact that in the Bible the metaphors and symbols of the Holy Spirit are often things: fire, wind, oil, water and dove. Of course, all these contain vital truths, and it is worth looking at them, if only briefly.

Fire

In Old Testament days, fire was quite often associated with a manifestation of God, a symbol of his holy presence. For example, there is God's appearance to Moses in the burning bush (Exodus 3: 2), the assurance of God's presence throughout the wilderness journey by the pillar of fire (Exodus 13: 21f.), the descending of God upon Mount Sinai (Exodus 19: 18), and the chariots of fire round about Elisha (2 Kings 6: 17).[4]

In the New Testament, John the Baptist said of Jesus, 'He will baptise you with the Holy Spirit and with fire. His winnowing fork is in his hand, to clear his threshing floor, and to gather the wheat into his granary, but the chaff he will burn with unquenchable fire' (Luke 3: 16–17). Notice the repetition of 'fire'. This indicates that John was thinking of the fire of God's holiness: the fire of God's Spirit would purify the believer, and the fire of God's judgment would destroy the unbeliever (chaff). The Spirit is the Holy Spirit: he comes not only to bring God's love and peace; he comes to burn up what is rotten, so as to make us more like Jesus. This, no doubt, will be a painful process, but God is not interested in second-class discipleship. He will not fill with his Holy Spirit a vessel that is unholy. Hence, the need of fire. Indeed at Pentecost, when the Spirit fell, 'tongues of fire' rested on each one of them.

[4] See also Deuteronomy 4: 11, 24; Ezekiel 1: 4, 13; Zechariah 13: 9 et al.

Wind

This speaks of the invigorating sovereignty of the Spirit of God. 'The wind blows where it wills, and you hear the sound of it, but you do not know whence it comes or whither it goes; so it is with every one who is born of the Spirit' (John 3: 8). And again, at Pentecost, 'suddenly a sound came from heaven like the rush of a mighty wind, and it filled all the house where they were sitting . . . And they were all filled with the Holy Spirit . . .' (Acts 2: 2, 4).

Dr. Coggan, preaching at the Lee Abbey Reunion in St. Paul's Cathedral in 1964, spoke of the wind and fire of the Spirit in these words:

How very alarming! Nature's two most devastating agents, wind and fire. Have you ever been in the path of a hurricane? Have you ever seen a beautiful structure razed by fire? If you have, you will not easily sentimentalise about these elements; and maybe you will think once again before you sing:

> *And His that gentle voice we hear,*
> *Soft as the breath of ev'n,*
> *That checks each thought, that calms each fear,*
> *And speaks of heaven.*

'Gentle'? It was a gale! 'Soft'? It blew to pieces their old and most cherished patterns of life! 'Checks each thought'? It stimulated them to such furious thinking that they could scarce get down on papyrus the ideas that came rushing to them! 'Speaks of heaven'? Maybe—but first of earth, with its pain and sin and ignorance; they found themselves blown into a perfect vortex of problems, to share them, to wrestle with them, to master them in the name of their Lord. True, the wind renewed, revived, freshened. But it also blew away the cobwebs and broke down the barriers. There was pain as well as joy in the experience of Pentecost.

Oil

This symbolises the anointing and healing of God's Spirit. In the Old Testament, Saul and Solomon were anointed with oil as a ceremonial recognition of their kingship (1 Samuel 10: 1; 1 Kings 1: 39). In the case of David, the association of oil and the Spirit is even more explicit: 'Then Samuel took the horn of oil, and anointed him in the midst of his brothers; and the Spirit of the Lord came mightily upon David from that day forward' (I Samuel 16: 13). Turning to the New Testament, James asks the question, 'Is any among you sick? Let him call for the elders of the church, and let them pray over him, anointing him with oil in the name of the Lord; and the prayer of faith will save the sick man, and the Lord will raise him up' (James 5: 14–15). Although it is sometimes argued that the use of oil here is purely for medicinal purposes (olive oil was used as a medicine both internally and externally), it is more probable that James intended that it should be a tangible sign of the Spirit's healing power.

I believe that the Church as a whole needs to study very carefully again the whole ministry of healing. I am not suggesting for one moment that God does not heal normally through medical science. But signs and wonders were, and still are, in some places today, part-and-parcel of the evangelism of the Church. Paul explained that his very fruitful ministry among the Gentiles was 'by word and deed, by the power of signs and wonders, by the power of the Holy Spirit' (Romans 15: 18–19). Remarkable ministries today show how effective healings can be in demonstrating that God is the living God.

Water

This indicates the regenerating and renewing power of the Holy Spirit. Jesus told the woman of Samaria about the living water which could become in her 'a spring of water welling up to eternal life' (John 4: 10–15); and later in the temple he gave this magnificent promise: 'If any one thirst, let him come to me and drink. He who believes in me, as the scripture has said, "Out of his heart shall flow rivers of living water." ' John goes on to comment, 'Now this he said about the Spirit . . .' (John 7: 37–39). Further, revival by the Spirit is graphically pictured in the Bible as pouring water on the thirsty land, and streams on the dry ground (Isaiah 44: 3; cf. 35: 6f. and Joel 2: 23). It is only the Holy Spirit who can quench the deepest thirst of the human heart, because it is only the Holy Spirit who can show us the beauty of Jesus and fill us with the love of God. Indeed, when we have drunk this glorious living water, it will spoil our thirst for everything else.

Dove

This symbolises the purity and peace of God's Spirit. 'And John bore witness, "I saw the Spirit descend as a dove from heaven, and it remained on him. I myself did not know him; but he who sent me to baptise with water said to me, 'He on whom you see the Spirit descend and remain, this is he who baptises with the Holy Spirit.' " ' (John 1 : 32–33).

All these symbols, beautiful and meaningful in themselves, are still 'things'. Partly because of this, many Christians speak wrongly of the Spirit as 'it'. It is therefore essential to remember that he is a person. 'If you think of him only as an influence,' said Dr. Torrey, 'you will be anxious that you may have more of it; but if you think of him as a person, you will desire that he may have more of you.'

HE BEARS THE MARKS OF A PERSON

In the New Testament he shows unmistakable qualities of thought, speech, action and feeling.

Thought
Paul speaks of the 'mind of the Spirit' (Romans 8 : 27); he intercedes for us and teaches us how to pray. Further, the Spirit can ' comprehend the thoughts of God' (1 Corinthians 2 : 11). In Acts 15 there is also a striking parallel. In verse 22 we read that 'it seemed good to the apostles and elders'; and in verse 28, 'it has seemed good to the Holy Spirit'. You cannot possibly say that with a depersonalised power or influence.

Speech
'The Holy Spirit spoke by the mouth of David ...' says Peter in Acts 1 : 16, which is incidentally an inter-

esting commentary on the inspiration of Scripture, as he quotes from Psalm 41 : 9. Again, 'the Spirit said to Philip, "Go up and join this chariot" ' (Acts 8 : 29), and this proved such effective guidance that it led directly to the conversion of the Ethiopian Chancellor of the Exchequer. Again, 'the Spirit expressly says . . .' wrote Paul to the young Timothy (1 Timothy 4 : 1), giving him a clear warning about 'deceitful spirits and doctrines of demons'. And in 1 Corinthians 2 : 13 Paul speaks of 'words taught by the Spirit'.

Action

In Acts 8 : 39 'the Spirit of the Lord caught up Philip', or 'snatched him away' (*N.E.B.* translation). Paul says that the sons of God are 'led by the Spirit' (Romans 8 : 14) and that the Spirit apportions gifts 'to each one individually as he wills' (1 Corinthians 12 : 11). Further, the Acts of the Apostles is one continuous testimony to the activity of the Spirit. We should not only pray that he will act in our midst today, but fully expect him to do so, providing of course that we fulfil the conditions for answered prayer. Of course there is always a sovereignty about the Spirit's action—'The wind blows where it wills' —but in the context of the gift of the Spirit, Jesus has encouraged us to ask, seek and knock (Luke 11 : 9–13).

Feeling

Paul speaks of 'the love of the Spirit' (Romans 15 : 30), and the Spirit crying out in our hearts 'Abba! Father!' (Galatians 4 : 6). Further, it is possible to grieve the Spirit (Ephesians 4 : 30), to lie to the Spirit (Acts 5 : 3–5), to quench the Spirit (1 Thessalonians

5: 19), and to blaspheme against the Spirit (Matthew 12: 31f.). Most of these expressions will be further developed later in this book, but it may be worth saying something about blasphemy against the Spirit.

Jesus said, 'Therefore I tell you, every sin and blasphemy will be forgiven men, but the blasphemy against the Spirit will not be forgiven. And whoever says a word against the Son of man will be forgiven; but whoever speaks against the Holy Spirit will not be forgiven, either in this age or in the age to come.' What is the meaning of this? Jesus had been acting in the power of the Spirit, but the Pharisees accused him of the work of the devil. In other words, they were refusing and rejecting God's gracious influence in the world by his Spirit through his Son. Now anyone can make mistakes. Therefore a careless and mistaken word spoken against the Son could still be forgiven. But a persistent and deliberate rejection of the Spirit could not be forgiven. God by his Spirit is always seeking to bring us his forgiveness and love. But if people persistently refuse God's forgiveness (offered by God's Spirit), those people cannot be forgiven, for they have rejected forgiveness. Sometimes I talk with those who are desperately afraid that they have committed the unforgivable sin. However, if a person is anxious about this, it is the clearest possible proof that the sin has not been committed. Anyone who has committed that sin would not be in the slightest degree anxious—rather thoroughly hardened by such persistent rejection.

This is abundantly clear in Christ's teaching about the Spirit in John 14–16, where the reference is constantly to 'he' and 'his'. For example, 'And when *he* comes, *he* will convince the world of sin and of righteousness and of judgment ... When the Spirit of truth comes, *he* will guide you into all the truth; for *he* will not speak on *his* own authority, but whatever *he* hears *he* will speak, and *he* will declare to you the things that are to come. *He* will glorify me, for *he* will take what is mine and declare it to you' (John 16: 8, 13–14). (Although some of these references are simply verbs in the third person singular, others are masculine pronouns.) This is all the more striking when the Greek word for Spirit is *Pneuma* (neuter).

However, I want to focus attention for a moment on John 14: 16-17: 'And I will pray the Father, and he will give you another Counsellor, to be with you for ever, even the Spirit of truth, whom the world cannot receive, because it neither sees him nor knows him; you know him, for he dwells with you, and will be in you.' Here there are four matters of particular interest.

First, the Spirit is a Counsellor (Paraklētos). Paraklētos is variously translated as Comforter, Divine Helper, Advocate, Lawyer, Intercessor, Strengthener, Standby. Literally, the word means 'one called alongside to help'. Therefore do not be deceived by the Authorised Version's 'Comforter'. The original meaning of 'Comforter' is something very different from what we imagine today. In the famous Bayeux tapestry, King

William is seen with a sword prodding one of his soldiers into battle. Underneath is this caption: 'King William comforteth his soldiers'! Indeed, in many ways the Holy Spirit is a very uncomfortable comforter: he shakes us out of our rut; he disturbs our complacency. He is as the wind and water and fire—the three most disconcerting elements.

Indeed, one could caricature the history of the Church in this way. The wind of the Spirit blows with revival power, and for a time all is exciting, if a little unpredictable. However, people come along and try to organise what is happening, because they want to be in control. In fact, they are frightened of not being in control. And the Holy Spirit sadly makes his departure. Sometimes, I think of it as God opening the windows of the Church. For a time there is a glorious fresh breeze, and the stuffiness disappears. However, the breeze begins to blow some of the forms and papers all over the place; and with such unseemly confusion, Church leaders firmly close the windows. The papers are once again arranged in the neat and orderly piles. But the windows are shut; the wind has gone, and the stuffiness returns. I am not suggesting that we should be careless or haphazard when it comes to efficiency. But all too often organisation can become a human substitute for genuine spiritual power.

Secondly, the Spirit is 'another Counsellor'. In the Greek, there are two main words for 'another': *allos* and *heteros*. Although these words are sometimes interchangeable, there is a subtle but important difference in the shade of meaning. *Heteros* means 'another, of a different kind'; *allos* means 'another, of the same

29

kind'. In John 14: 16 the Holy Spirit is *allos Parakletos*. Jesus is one Counsellor, wonderful and glorious, as the disciples immediately discovered; but the Spirit is another of the same kind. 'For the Spirit searches everything, even the depths of God.'

Thirdly, the Spirit is the 'Spirit of truth'. The combination and balance of Spirit and truth is very important. Paul, in describing the Christian's armour in Ephesians 6, writes, 'Take the sword of the Spirit, which is the word of God' (verse 17). The word without the Spirit is dead; and in some circles there is a terrifying orthodoxy: all the doctrines and phrases are there, but no life! On the other hand, spiritual experiences without the word are dangerous. No one can say that the Holy Spirit is dangerous, because he is the Spirit of God. But every Christian is liable to make mistakes, and Satan is the great deceiver, the father of lies. Therefore, spiritual experiences in themselves may, or may not, come from the Holy Spirit. That is why God has given us a clear objective test in the Scriptures. All spiritual experiences that we may have, or may seek after, must be according to the truth of God's word if they come from God's Spirit; he is the Spirit of truth. And in this 'feelings generation', the balance is tremendously important. Most people today will reject outright a dry orthodoxy. What is the reality of God, if we have no experience of him? However, religious experiences abound, and in themselves prove nothing, unless they are tested by the God-given test of his word.

Jesus also promised that the Spirit of truth 'will guide you into all the truth' (John 16: 13). One of the greatest hindrances to spiritual renewal is too great a dependence on people. We may ask, 'What does this Christian say? What does that preacher say?' Or else we may reject a new work of the Spirit by insisting that 'I was never taught that before; therefore it cannot be right!' We cling to traditional interpretations of God's word without thinking for ourselves under the guidance of the Spirit. Of course, often these traditional interpretations will be extremely helpful, especially when they come from those who have carefully studied the Scriptures for many years. After all, it is the Spirit himself who gives teachers, pastors and evangelists to the Church and who uses them to build up the body of Christ, 'so that we may no longer be children, tossed to and fro and carried about with every wind of doctrine' (Ephesians 4: 11–14). Here is the Spirit of truth working through those whom he has chosen for the benefit of the whole body. Nevertheless, no-one, however godly, has a monopoly of Biblical understanding. No person is given to the Church to guide us into all the truth. That is the sovereign work of the Spirit of God; and if we put people into his place, we may very soon be guilty of the error of the Pharisees who made void the word of God through their tradition. Always we should be asking, humbly but urgently, not 'What does so-and-so say?' but 'What is God saying by his Spirit?' He is the only one who can guide us into all the truth.

After all, most of us, in our natural human smallness and weakness, tend to concentrate on certain emphases of doctrine at the expense of others. That is why we have so many definable groups which we label so quickly: Calvinists, Arminians, Pentecostals,

Neo-Pentecostals, a variety of groups which stress Holiness, or the Return of Christ, or the Millennium. Some stress the mind; others emphasise experience; some concentrate on evangelism; others major on social action. All this perhaps is inevitable. The tragedy comes when we insist that our group is right and that other groups are wrong. Certainly, there is only one gospel that saves, and there must be no woolly thinking about that: 'If any one is preaching to you a gospel contrary to that which you received, let him be accursed,' wrote Paul in Galatians 1: 9. But beyond that there may be a great variation of emphasis within the whole counsel of God. It is only the Spirit who can guide us into all the truth; and undoubtedly he will, from time to time, correct a wrong emphasis here, or add something that is missing there—providing that, throughout our lives, we are open-minded and willing to be taught by the Spirit of God from the word of God.

Fourthly, the Spirit is not understood by the world. 'The world cannot receive [him], because it neither sees him nor knows him.' Until a person has a spiritual rebirth, there is a complete failure to understand the Holy Spirit. 'The unspiritual man does not receive the gifts of the Spirit of God, for they are folly to him, and he is not able to understand them because they are spiritually discerned' (1 Corinthians 2: 14). One clear mark of the various cults is their misunderstanding of the Holy Spirit. For example, Jehovah's Witnesses think of the Spirit as any power which God might exercise, and the Spirit is written with a small 's' in their Bible. Christadelphians also speak of the

Spirit as purely the active force radiating from God. Mormons think of the Spirit as a substance like electricity. Swedenborgianism thinks of the Spirit as an influence.

However, we have already seen something of the forceful way in which the Holy Spirit is spoken of as the Third Person of the Godhead. Many Scriptures, apart from John 14–16, would underline this. Jesus told his disciples to baptise people 'in the name of the Father and of the Son and of the Holy Spirit' (Matthew 28: 19). Paul ends his second letter to the Corinthians by praying that 'the grace of the Lord Jesus Christ and the love of God and the fellowship of the Holy Spirit be with you all' (2 Corinthians 13: 14). Peter tells his Christian readers that they are 'chosen and destined by God the Father and sanctified by the Spirit for obedience to Jesus Christ ...' (1 Peter 1: 2). Jude exhorts his readers to 'pray in the Holy Spirit; keep yourselves in the love of God; wait for the mercy of our Lord Jesus Christ ...' (Jude 20–21). Repeatedly, we see the Biblical revelation of 'Three Persons and One God'.

If we find it hard to understand this, we must remember that we are talking about an infinite personal God who is, by definition, infinitely beyond our total finite understanding. We are therefore dependent on his self-revelation, particularly through the Scriptures; and it is a profound mistake to 'reduce' God to the level of our own minds. Even Paul, soaked in the Scriptures and enriched by vivid personal revelations, cried out, 'O the depth of the riches and wisdom and knowledge of God! How unsearchable

33

are his judgments and how inscrutable his ways!'
(Romans 11 : 33).

THE WORK OF THE HOLY SPIRIT

In this chapter I shall confine myself to three general
truths.

First, the Spirit creates life. He was active in the creation
of the world, when we are told that 'the Spirit of God
was moving over the face of the waters' (Genesis
1: 2). He was also present in the creation of humanity,
when 'God breathed into his nostrils the breath of
life; and man became a living being' (Genesis 2: 7).
Although the word 'Spirit' (*ruach*) is not used here,
it is certainly implied. Indeed in the Old Testament
'Spirit', 'breath' and 'wind' are almost interchangeable.
This is seen most vividly in the famous vision of the
valley of dry bones in Ezekiel 37. 'Then he said to me,
"Prophesy to the breath, prophesy, son of man, and
say to the breath (or *wind* or *spirit*—marginal reading), Thus says the Lord God: Come from the four
winds, O breath, and breathe, and breathe upon these
slain, that they may live" ' (verse 9). And five verses
further on God explains to Ezekiel the interpretation
of this vision: 'I will put my Spirit within you, and
you shall live ...' The Psalmist, too, declares that
when 'thou takest away their breath, they die and
return to their dust. When thou sendest forth thy
Spirit, they are created' (Psalm 104: 29–30).

The Holy Spirit is also active in *new* creation, or
regeneration. We shall consider this further in Chapter 2, but Jesus told Nicodemus of the vital need to

be 'born of water and the Spirit', for 'that which is born of the flesh is flesh, and that which is born of the Spirit is spirit' (John 3: 1–8).

Without the Spirit of God, then, there is no life—neither physical life nor spiritual life. He is the author and giver of life.

Therefore, in any Christian church or fellowship, there is no real life unless the Spirit is active in power. Modern methods of communication, imaginative strategies for evangelism, well-known speakers, well-planned programmes, are no substitute at all for the vital breath of the Spirit of God. Dr. A. W. Tozer once wrote:

> The only power God recognises in his Church is the power of his Spirit; whereas the only power actually recognised today by the majority of evangelicals is the power of man. God does his work by the operation of the Spirit, while Christian leaders attempt to do theirs by the power of the trained and devoted intellect. Bright personality has taken the place of the divine afflatus. Everything that men do in their own strength and by means of their own abilities is done for time alone; the quality of eternity is not in it. Only what is done through the Eternal Spirit will abide eternally; all else is wood, hay, stubble. It is a solemn thought that some of us who fancy ourselves to be important evangelical leaders may find at last we have been but busy harvesters of stubble.[5]

Secondly, the Spirit glorifies Christ. 'When the Coun-

---

[5] *The Holy Spirit is Indispensable* (Reprint leaflet from The Alliance Witness).

sellor comes,' said Jesus, 'he will bear witness to me . . .
He will glorify me, for he will take what is mine and
declare it to you' (John 15: 26; 16: 14). This is an extremely important statement, for it is always the work
of the Spirit to exalt and magnify the Lord Jesus Christ.
He will help Christians to honour Christ in their
lives, to love and serve Christ in every way they can,
to bear witness to Christ in an unbelieving world that
is lost without him. He will reveal our completeness
in Christ, the sovereignty of Christ, the finished work
of Christ and the fact that God has blessed us with
every spiritual blessing in Christ. Alford once com-
mented on John 16: 14 in this way: 'This verse is
decisive against all additions and pretended revelations, subsequent to and beside Christ; it being the
work of the Spirit to testify to the things of Christ,
and not to anything new or beyond him.' Therefore
a good test for any claim for a new work of the Spirit
is this: Is Christ glorified? Is Christ at the centre? If
Christians claim some blessing of the Spirit, have
they a new love for Jesus, a new hunger for his word,
a new desire to tell others about him? These are the
crucial issues; and personal experiences without these
Christ-centred consequences are either meaningless or
counterfeit.

Thirdly, the Spirit unites believers. 'For just as the
body is one and has many members, and all the members of the body, though many, are one body, so it is
with Christ. For by one Spirit we were all baptised
into one body—Jews or Greeks, slave or free—and all
were made to drink of one Spirit' (1 Corinthians 12:
12–13). Notice two points of particular relevance

about these verses, in their context. In the first place, this is the outstanding chapter in the Bible on the gifts of the Spirit (see verses 4–11, 27–31). But it is also the outstanding chapter on our unity in Christ, created by the Holy Spirit. Therefore, when the gifts of the Spirit are rightly manifested, in the atmosphere of love (1 Corinthians 13), there are no problems. In fact, the gifts should increase the love and unity of the fellowship, not the reverse: 'To each is given the manifestation of the Spirit for the common good' (verse 7). If, then, the gifts cause division in a fellowship, there is something else (other than the gifts, unless of course the gifts are counterfeit) that is radically wrong: either on the part of those who have the gifts, or on the part of those who do not. It is the Holy Spirit who both bestows the gifts and unites believers. Thus the gifts of the Spirit cannot, by themselves, bring disunity. The fear that 'the gifts will split the fellowship' is a misguided fear. Division may be caused only by the way in which these gifts are received or rejected. We shall look at this in more detail in Chapter 3.

In the second place, since the Holy Spirit is concerned to unite Christians, it is both ironical and tragic that there should be any split in any fellowship about any aspect of the Holy Spirit. The trouble is usually this: we fail to appreciate the sovereignty of the Spirit of God. We have preconceived ideas of the way in which the Spirit must work; and when he cuts across those ideas (as he nearly always does in times of renewal and revival) there will be some who do not like what he is doing. Others fortunately welcome the new life, being patient with the inevitable teething-troubles. 'When the Holy Spirit comes on men and women,' said Dr. Coggan in a recorded interview,[6] 'there is new life; there is often disorder, too, untidy edges. But give me this every time if otherwise I have to put up with cold, lifeless orthodoxy!'

Further, we must never forget this: if, on a point of doctrine or practice, I happen to be right and others wrong, and if at the same time I have no love, then *I am nothing* in the sight of God. Whenever there is new spiritual life which is mixed with disorder and untidiness, love must win the day. And, in love, all of us need to remain wide open to all that God wants to teach us and give us by his Spirit, to the glory of his Son.

[6] *Church of England Newspaper*, March 5th, 1971, p. 4.

CHAPTER 2

THE HOLY SPIRIT IN THE INDIVIDUAL

ALREADY we have seen that the desperate need of the Church today is the Holy Spirit. 'Nothing else will save our Church from its spiritual torpor or our country from lapsing into complete paganism,' as John Stott once said. However, every cry for spiritual revival or renewal must include the prayer, 'Lord, begin in me.' Therefore, the personal activity of the Holy Spirit is of immense importance, and it is partly in this direction that a measure of confusion exists today.

As a starting-point, it is perhaps necessary to stress that the believer has potentially everything in Christ. Paul begins his magnificent letter to the Ephesians with this burst of praise: 'Blessed be the God and Father of our Lord Jesus Christ, who has blessed us in Christ with every spiritual blessing in the heavenly places' (Ephesians 1 : 3). If we are in Christ, it is all there. We are heirs of God and joint heirs with Christ. Indeed the Spirit 'is the guarantee of our inheritance until we acquire possession of it' (verse 14).

Let us briefly look at four aspects of the Spirit's work in the life of the individual.

Here there is at least a threefold activity of the Holy Spirit.

First, he convicts of sin. 'I will send him to you,' said Jesus. 'And when he comes, he will convince the world of sin and of righteousness and of judgment: of sin, because they do not believe in me; of righteousness, because I go to the Father, and you will see me no more; of judgment, because the ruler of this world is judged' (John 16: 7–11). Notice that Jesus stressed that the coming of the Spirit upon the disciples would be an essential step to the conviction of the world: 'I will send him to *you*. And when he comes [i.e. to *you*] he will convince the *world* ...' But the world will never be convinced of sin, righteousness and judgment until the Holy Spirit comes with power on those who are believers. It is partly the absence of such power and reality in the Church that leads directly to such open and unashamed sin in the world. In some Christian circles there is far too much self-righteous disapproval of the ways of the world, when all along the reason for this lies with God's own people: 'If my people who are called by my name humble themselves, and pray and seek my face, and turn from their wicked ways, then I will hear from heaven and will forgive their sin and heal their land' (2 Chronicles 7: 14). Certainly, when there is a mighty visitation of the Spirit in times of revival, bringing great conviction of sin within the community, the prelude to this has nearly always been Christians getting right with God. Those who know Christ must take sin seriously before those who do not.

A vivid illustration of this is the case of the Hebrides revival in 1949. Just before the revival came, a number of men agreed that on three nights of the week they would meet together in a barn in the village of Sharda to pray for a spiritual awakening. Duncan Campbell has described it in these words: 'For months they waited upon God in this manner. Nothing happened, until one night ... one young man, taking his Bible in his hand, read from Psalm 24, "Who shall ascend the hill of God and who shall stand in his holy presence? He that hath clean hands and a pure heart, who hath not lifted up his soul unto vanity nor sworn deceitfully; he shall receive the blessing of the Lord." He shut his Bible and, looking down at his companions, said this, "Brethren, it seems to me just so much humbug waiting as we are waiting, praying as we are praying, unless we ourselves are rightly related to God." He then began to pray, and in his prayer he asked God to reveal to him if his hands were clean, if his heart was pure ... At that moment, something happened in that barn. A power was let loose that shook the parish from centre to circumference ... God had visited them and neither they nor the parish could ever be the same again.'[1]

In particular Jesus in John 16 describes the areas in which the Spirit will convince the world. First, he will convince 'of sin, because they do not believe in me'. Jesus is God's greatest gift to the world, and therefore not to believe in him is the greatest sin. That is why we have that striking statement in John 3: 18: 'He who believes in him is not condemned; he who does

[1] Tape-recorded talk.

not believe is condemned already.' There can be no forgiveness for such an unbeliever, and it is therefore the work of the Holy Spirit to bring home the seriousness of rejecting Christ. Sin is not just theft, murder and adultery. It is an attitude of rebellion against God. It is breaking God's commandments, ignoring God's warnings, rejecting God's mercy, not believing on God's Son. A prominent member of the community told me recently that although for many years he had been a good churchman, now for the first time he had come into a living relationship with Jesus Christ. What had happened? During a morning service in his church, the Spirit had convicted him of the sin of not believing, in the sense of personal commitment, in Jesus.

Secondly, the Spirit will convince the world 'of righteousness, because I go to the Father, and you will see me no more'. In other words, the Spirit will convince men and women of the rightness of Jesus Christ: that he is the Son of God, that he is the Saviour of the world, that he alone is the way to God, that he alone can bring us to God—there is no other! A young art teacher told me that often he had argued with Christians against the deity of Jesus; but one Sunday, listening to an evangelistic sermon, he was suddenly convinced of the truth of Jesus. This was the convincing work of the Spirit of God.

Thirdly, the Spirit will convince people 'of judgment, because the ruler of this world is judged'. Men and women therefore will be convinced that Christ has won the victory over sin and Satan, that he has supreme authority over all, and that he will come again in power to judge the living and the dead. The seventy disciples came back to Jesus from their first mission in great excitement: 'Lord even the demons are subject to us in your name!' (Luke 10: 17). Here was a thrilling foretaste of the triumph of Jesus Christ over all the power of the enemy; and it is the Spirit's sovereign work to make this triumph real in terms of our experience.

Further, since the world must be convinced first of the sin of not believing in Jesus, secondly of the righteousness and truth about Jesus, and thirdly of the judgment of Satan by Jesus, the more we preach Jesus and witness to Jesus, the better the Holy Spirit is able to do his convincing work. This is clearly what Paul felt in the largely pagan and permissive atmosphere of Corinth. Some Jews there were always demanding more signs and more evidence, while the Greeks were constantly pursuing the high-sounding but empty wisdom of the world. However 'we preach Christ crucified', wrote Paul, 'a stumbling-block to Jews and folly to Gentiles, but to those who are called, both Jews and Greeks, Christ the power of God and the wisdom of God'. Indeed his concern was to 'know nothing among you except Jesus Christ and him crucified' so that there might be a 'demonstration of the Spirit and power, [and] that your faith might not rest in the wisdom of men but in the power of God' (1 Corinthians 1: 23–24; 2: 2–5).

Secondly, the Spirit causes the new birth. 'Unless one is born of water and the Spirit, he cannot enter the Kingdom of God,' said Jesus; and he went on to explain why: 'That which is born of the flesh is flesh, and that which is born of the Spirit is spirit' (John

43

3: 5–6). There is no substitute at all for this sovereign regenerating work of the Spirit of God.

The Rev. Charles Jarman, rector of a large and prosperous episcopal church in the United States, with several university degrees in theology to his name, wrote this: 'I preached for fifty-two years before I knew the Lord Jesus as my personal Saviour. True, I was a minister and thought I was a Christian, but that did not make me one.' And in the story of his life he records how on March 28th, 1966, he knelt down and for the first time asked Christ to come into his life. 'I have never felt such peace . . . I knew that I was born again in Christ Jesus.'

We must never devalue the miracle of the new birth. In Kathryn Kuhlman's book *I Believe in Miracles* there are fascinating and astonishing records of twenty-one healing miracles: cancer, leukaemia, paralysis, sclerosis—the lot! But constantly, she re-iterates the point that the greatest miracle of them all is the new birth by the Spirit of God. The Jewish philosopher Martin Buber once asked, 'Is there any force in the world that can change that intractable thing, human nature? There's a tragedy at the heart of things.' There is no force in the world that can cause a positive revolution in the very nature of humanity. That is one of the most obvious facts in this century of political and social revolutions. 'Revolution transforms everything except the human heart.' It is only the Holy Spirit of God that can transform that, by the process of spiritual rebirth.

Thirdly, the Spirit witnesses to our salvation. 'When we cry, "Abba, Father!" it is the Spirit himself bearing witness with our spirit that we are children of God' (Romans 8: 15–16). One thing I like most about going away from home is coming back again! My two children rush out and jump into my arms. 'Daddy! Daddy!' they cry, and for a few moments we have a delightful love-in. It is always a great moment, however exasperating they can be at other times. The Holy Spirit creates within us the same spontaneous cry of a child to the heavenly Father: 'Abba! Daddy! Father!' In other words the Spirit gives us an inward assurance about our relationship with God, a deep confidence that he is our Father and that we are his children. Once we are sure about this, it transforms every aspect of our Christian life. Paul, in Romans 8, after referring to the witness of the Spirit, goes on to talk about suffering. But for him, suffering is not a huge stumbling-block to faith. Rather, he considers that 'the sufferings of this present time are not worth comparing with the glory that is to be revealed to us.' He is absolutely sure that nothing at all 'will be able to separate us from the love of God in Christ Jesus our Lord' (verses 18, 38–39). Why is he so convinced about these things? It is because of the witness of the Spirit in his heart. This is more than a mental acceptance of gospel truths. It is more than an intellectual agreement with doctrinal statements. It is a profound, inward, personal knowledge of the father–child relationship—a 'heart-knowledge' that only the Spirit can give.

Much has been written about this 'witness of the Spirit'. The important point to grasp is that it is distinguishable from our own witness concerning our salvation. I may believe the promises of God, trust in the cross of Christ and see something of the new life springing up due to the work of the Holy Spirit; but all this is the witness of my spirit that I am a child of God. However valid this may be, Paul is talking here of 'a witness given *to* us as distinct from the witness given *by* us ... It is to us indeed the witness is given and it is "to our spirit".'[2] This witness cannot be clearly defined, but is undoubtedly experienced, and gives believers a profound conviction that they belong to God, so that they cry out 'Abba! Father!'

THE INSTRUCTION OF THE CHRISTIAN

For this the Holy Spirit plays an indispensable twofold role.

First, there is revelation. God is a God of revelation. We should all be incurably agnostic if that were not so. We do not even know what is going on in each other's minds, apart from the way we express or reveal our thoughts, usually by our words. Is there then a word of God? Has God spoken? Has God revealed himself? The Christian contention is that God has indeed revealed himself, through the Jewish nation, through the Scriptures, and supremely through his Son. 'In many and various ways God spoke of old to our fathers by the prophets; but in these last days he has spoken to us by a Son' (Hebrews 1: 1–2). And Peter, speaking about Old Testament prophecy, wrote this: 'No prophecy of scripture is a matter of one's

[2] *The Epistle of Paul to the Romans*, by John Murray; Marshall, Morgan and Scott, p. 297. See also the exposition by Robert Haldane, op. cit., *ad loc.*

own interpretation, because no prophecy ever came by the impulse of man, but men moved by the Holy Spirit spoke from God' (2 Peter 1: 20–21). The word 'moved' (*pheromenoi*) is a particularly interesting one: it occurs in Acts 27: 15 and 17 to describe a ship 'driven' by the wind. This gives a helpful picture of God's revelation through the Scriptures. A ship driven by the wind still retains its own character, but is entirely dependent on the power of the wind. Similarly the prophets of God retained their own individual characters (Amos is very different from Hosea, who is quite unlike Daniel), but were entirely dependent on the inspiration of the Spirit. They hoisted their sails, by being receptive and obedient to the Spirit of God, and consequently the Holy Spirit filled their sails and drove their craft along in the direction he wished.

This also gives an insight of the activity of the Holy Spirit in our lives today. Although undoubtedly he takes the initiative in our lives, bringing conviction of sin, drawing us to Christ, prompting us into some line of action, working within us both to will and to work for God's good pleasure, he seldom forces us to do anything. Normally he waits for us to leave the static security of the harbour, to hoist our sails and to be willing to be used in any direction that he wills. Some Christians are frightened to do this, because they are not sure of what might happen. They remain safe, but firmly anchored, never making any real progress.

God, then, has revealed himself through the Scriptures. This is not to say that this is the only way in which he can speak to us today, but it is the primary

47

means; and this must therefore be the standard and test for everything else. God has always spoken to people, since the beginnings of creation, in a great variety of ways; and he is still doing so today. But he has chosen a careful selection of his self-revelation as our supreme authority for belief and behaviour, and all other matters must bow to this authority. Christ made this very clear in his day when he brought both the traditionalists (Pharisees) and the rationalists (Sadducees) to heel by reminding them of the authority of the Scriptures: 'Is not this why you are wrong, that you know neither the scriptures nor the power of God' (Mark 12: 24; *cf.* 7: 6–13; Matthew 22: 29).

Secondly, there is illumination. 'As it is written, "What no eye has seen, nor ear heard, nor the heart of man conceived, what God has prepared for those who love him," God has revealed to us through the Spirit. For the Spirit searches everything, even the depths of God ... No one comprehends the thoughts of God except the Spirit of God. Now we have received ... the Spirit which is from God, that we might understand the gifts bestowed on us by God ... The unspiritual man does not receive the gifts of the Spirit of God, for they are folly to him, and he is not able to understand them because they are spiritually discerned' (1 Corinthians 2: 9–14).

A young man knelt with me in my room one evening to ask Christ to enter his life. Later he wrote to me this letter: 'All I can say now is that "before" I was completely blind and could not see what God was offering me all the time ... I am so glad that now I know that Christ is real and alive, and I want you to share this joy with me.'

One of the most outstanding illustrations of this
essential illumination by the Holy Spirit is the case of
William Haslam, who was converted by his own sermon, while preaching in the pulpit! Let Haslam, a
nineteenth-century vicar in Cornwall, tell his own
story:

I went into the pulpit and gave my text ... I do
not remember all I said, but I felt a wonderful light
and joy coming into my soul ... Whether it was
something in my words, or my manner, or my look,
I know not; but all of a sudden a local preacher, who
happened to be in the congregation, stood up, and
putting up his arms, shouted out in Cornish manner, 'The parson is converted! the parson is converted! Hallelujah!' and in another moment his
voice was lost in the shouts and praises of three or
four hundred of the congregation. Instead of rebuk-
ing this extraordinary 'brawling', as I should have
done in a former time, I joined in the outburst of
praise; and to make it more orderly, I gave out the
Doxology—'Praise God, from whom all blessings
flow'—and the people sang it with heart and voice,
over and over again. My Churchmen were dismayed,
and many of them fled precipitately from the place.
Still the voice of praise went on, and was swelled by
numbers of passers-by, who came into the church,
greatly surprised to hear and see what was going on.
When this subsided, I found at least twenty people
crying for mercy, whose voices had not been heard
in the excitement and noise of thanksgiving. They
all professed to find peace and joy in believing.

Amongst this number there were three from my own house; and we returned home praising God.[3]

Further, all spiritual truths must be taught by the Spirit. Today, many Christians are Bible-taught, but not Spirit-taught.

For a man to understand revealed truth requires an act of God equal to the original act which inspired the text, [wrote Dr. A. W. Tozer.] There is such a thing as a gift of knowing, a gift that comes from heaven. The textualism of our times is based upon the same premise as the old-line rationalism, confidence in the ability of the human mind to do that which the Bible declares it was never created to do and consequently is wholly incapable of doing.

Repeatedly, I have found it one thing to grasp a Biblical truth in my mind, but quite another thing to understand it in my spirit. Intellectually, I may know what it says and may believe it to be true; but spiritually I may still fail to 'see' it. The great preacher, Dr. R. W. Dale, records that while preparing an Easter sermon, he suddenly saw the wonder of the resurrection of Christ: 'Christ is alive! Alive! living as really as I am myself! It came upon me as a burst of sudden glory. Christ is living! My people shall know it.' There is no doubt that not only had he understood the resurrection of Christ before this moment; he also had believed it, preached it and taught it for many years. But suddenly he 'saw' it with

[3] *From Death into Life*, by W. Haslam; Morgan and Scott, p. 48.

this burst of sudden glory. Here is the exciting illumination of the Spirit, who can make even 'old' truths wonderfully fresh and new.

THE DAILY LIFE OF THE CHRISTIAN

Here, trying to be selective is almost impossible, because the Holy Spirit should increasingly influence every area of the life of the believer: relationships, home life, artistic expression, personal habits and so forth. However, it is important to look briefly at three aspects of his influence.

First, temptation and victory. 'The law of the Spirit of life in Christ Jesus has set me free from the law of sin and death' (Romans 8: 2). Imagine that you are holding a book on the palm of your hand. If the book is steady, it is kept in place by two equal and opposite forces: the force of gravity pulling it down and the force of your hand keeping it up. Remove your hand, and at once the book falls to the ground. Raise your hand, and the book of course goes with it. In the same way, there is the downward pull in our life of the 'law of sin and death'. Without the Spirit of life in Christ Jesus we have no strength to overcome this 'sin and death' which pulls us down. However, the Spirit within us can overcome this downward law; and providing we rely on his strength, and not on our own, we can rise up victorious.

The important thing is for us to admit our weakness and helplessness: 'I know that nothing good dwells within me, that is, in my flesh. I can will what is right but I cannot do it ... Wretched man that I am! Who

51

will deliver me from this body of death? Thanks be to God through Jesus Christ our Lord!' (Romans 7: 18, 24–25). Notice how Paul burst out into thanksgiving and praise. His own natural weakness has not been changed at all. But he praises God that he has the answer through Jesus Christ and through the Spirit of life in Christ Jesus.

Praise is one of the great secrets of victory. Paul not only says, 'Give thanks *in* all circumstances' (1 Thessalonians 5: 18) but 'always and *for* everything giving thanks' (Ephesians 5: 20). As soon as we praise God *for* our battles, trials and temptations, we are allowing him to work through those problems, for we are declaring our confidence that 'in everything God works for good with those who love him' (Romans 8: 28).

I remember talking to a Christian woman whose marriage was on the rocks. Either she would leave her husband, she told me, or commit suicide, or both. Life was totally bleak and desperate. After a time I suggested two things: first, she must repent of her bitter, critical spirit, however understandable it might seem in the situation (it is our reaction to our situation, not the situation itself, which is always our biggest problem); secondly, she must thank God *for* the problem itself. This, she said, she could not possibly do. But I showed her Romans 8: 28 and Ephesians 5: 20; and explained that the strain and tensions in her marriage were driving her, not up against a brick wall, but into the arms of Jesus. Within a few minutes she knelt in my study, repented of her bitterness, and thanked God for the crisis in her marriage. From that time onwards, her relationship with her husband improved beyond recognition. The Spirit of life in Christ Jesus had set her free.

Secondly, prayer. Most Christians, if not all, find real prayer incredibly difficult. Indeed, there is nothing more difficult in the Christian life, because there is nothing more powerful or spiritual than prayer. Worship and adoration is perhaps the hardest of all. Therefore in this realm especially we need the direct help of the Holy Spirit: 'Likewise the Spirit helps us in our weakness; for we do not know how to pray as we ought, but the Spirit himself intercedes for us with sighs too deep for words. And he who searches the hearts of men knows what is the mind of the Spirit, because the Spirit intercedes for the saints according to the will of God' (Romans 8: 26f.).

If you find prayer dull and difficult, be still before God. Find that position of peace and rest. Shut the door on the outside world. Then specifically ask for the Holy Spirit's help and guidance. We are to learn to 'pray at all times in the Spirit, with all prayer and supplication' (Ephesians 6: 18). Hoist your sails! After that, launch out, trusting that the Spirit will give you increasing joy and liberty. As in the area of temptation and victory, it is a very good practice to begin with a 'sacrifice of praise', whether you feel like it or not. Read a psalm of praise; sing a hymn or a chorus of praise. Worship the Lord. Fix your mind on him, his glory and majesty, his beauty and strength. 'One thing have I asked of the Lord, that I will seek after; that I may dwell in the house of the Lord all the days of my life, to behold the beauty of the Lord, and to inquire in his temple' (Psalm 27: 4). 'Worthy art thou, our Lord and God, to receive glory and honour and power ...' (Revelation 4: 11). As we praise and worship like this, our vision of him brightens, our faith grows, and prayer at once becomes more meaningful. Dull prayer is usually rushed prayer: we rush into God's presence and ask for this and that. But God will not respond to our haste. He waits for our love and adoration, so that he might pour his love into our hearts through the Holy Spirit. Only then do we really begin to communicate. Confession, supplication—all these will follow as we consciously seek his face.

Thirdly, guidance. There are few matters which cause such confusion as this. No one finds guidance easy, for in part it depends on an ever-deepening relationship with God himself; and it is the very difficulties of guidance that cast us back on him again and again. It is part of fallen human nature that we sometimes want to use God, as we might use a computer: feed in the question, and out comes the answer! But we can never use God; it is God who wants to use us. And he can do this only when we are in an attitude of total dependence, when we love him with all our heart, mind, soul and strength.

However, the more sensitive a Christian may be to the work of the Holy Spirit, the more tantalising are such passages as Acts 8: 'the Spirit said to Philip, "Go up and join this chariot" ' (verse 29); or Acts 13: 'While they were worshipping the Lord and fasting, the Holy Spirit said, "Set apart for me Barnabas and Saul ..." ' (verses 2-4). Further, Christian biography is liberally sprinkled with unusual and remarkable guidance by the Holy Spirit.

How, then, are we to distinguish a genuine prompting of the Spirit of God from personal desires or even Satanic counterfeit? How freely should we use the expression, 'The Lord told me to say this, or do that'? When is it right to claim divine authority for our words or actions? 'Do not ascribe to God what is not of God,' wrote John Wesley. 'Do not easily suppose dreams, voices, impressions, visions, revelations to be from God without sufficient evidence. They may be purely natural; they may be diabolical. Therefore, remember the caution of the apostle, "Beloved, believe not every spirit, but try the spirits whether they be of God." Try all things by the written Word, and let all bow down before it.'

Clearly, hasty claims for divine guidance can lead to much abuse and dishonour to God himself. You may know of the young man who went, somewhat against his will, to a retreat where there was prolonged and concentrated meditation. One afternoon he planned his escape into the town; but as he crept along the corridor he met the conductor of the retreat. 'Where are you going?' 'Well, sir, the Holy Spirit moved me to go into the town to do some shopping,' replied the young man as he tried to sound very spiritual. 'Then of course you must go,' said the conductor of the retreat, without batting an eyelid. 'But I hope that both of you know that it's early closing!'

There are two opposite mistakes about guidance. The first is an over-eager desire to ascribe almost every prompting and feeling to the direct intervention of the Holy Spirit. This mistake may arise from either pride or unbelief or both. Out of pride, Christians may be tempted to claim special revelations and unusual guidance, which gives the impression that they are 'more spiritual' than other Christians; and in their unbelief they feel the need to *prove to themselves* the activity of the Spirit in their lives. Not being quite sure of the Spirit's presence and power, they are over-anxious for signs and wonders to demonstrate that the Spirit is at work after all.

The second mistake is to deny all such activity of the Spirit, reducing guidance to that much overworked phrase 'sanctified commonsense'. Of course, God frequently works in a way that our mind understands and accepts, especially if that mind has been influenced by the word of God and prayer. At the same time, 'My thoughts are not your thoughts, neither are your ways my ways, says the Lord' (Isaiah 55: 8); and many illustrations of faith in the Bible show God's blessing on those who act on his often remarkable guidance, instead of relying on their common sense. To deny God's direct leading by his Holy Spirit is to deny the sovereign action of the Spirit in the lives of people today. Certainly the Spirit will never say anything contrary to the written word of God, but God is a living God. He *has* spoken and he *still* speaks. There should be a continuous living relationship between the Father and his children, in whom the Spirit dwells.

How, then, does God guide us? Basically, there are four main strands, and when all four are woven together our conviction about that guidance may be very strong. If only one strand is present, we should probably wait for further confirmation. What are these four strands?

First, God guides through *circumstances*. 'And when they had come opposite Mysia, they attempted to go into Bithynia, but the Spirit of Jesus did not allow them' (Acts 16: 10). We must stress that we do not know for certain here how the Spirit stopped them, but undoubtedly God does at times 'close doors' on certain possibilities. We try to do something, but, for one reason or another, the way is blocked. On the other hand, a sudden opportunity may present itself. Unexpectedly the door swings open, the way seems clear. And it may be that the Spirit is guiding us through these open and closed doors. Further, when God has opened a door, we must take care that we do not close it ourselves in favour of something that seems more attractive. Students at university or college should never pull out of their courses, claiming guidance, unless they not only are deeply convinced about it themselves but have received confirmation of this through other means of guidance as well. With very few and rare exceptions, God wants us to complete what we have started: 'Whatever your task, work heartily, as serving the Lord' (Colossians 3: 23).

Secondly, God guides through *other Christians*. In Acts 6 'the whole multitude' of believers chose the seven deacons. In Acts 13 the Holy Spirit spoke through the Church about Barnabas and Saul. In that instance it was a direct word of prophecy; but it is worth pointing out that this prophecy probably acted as a confirmation of guidance already received: 'The Holy Spirit said, "Set apart for me Barnabas and Saul for the work to which I have called them"' (verse 2). The Spirit had already called them, and therefore the prophecy simply confirmed that calling. We should always be wary of other Christians getting the guidance for us, especially if through a claimed word of prophecy. This certainly must be tested. .

On the other hand, our own personal convictions, however strong and deep, should equally be open to the prayerful opinions of others. If the guidance is genuine, nothing will be lost; but this procedure is an important safeguard against spurious promptings. And remember, that 'the wisdom from above is first pure, then peaceable, gentle, open to reason' (James 3: 17). The Christian who will not listen to reason is a fool. If we close our minds to what God might well be saying to us through other Christians we are no less than bigots, and bigotry has no place in the pure, peaceable, gentle and reasonable operation of the Holy Spirit. Of course, there is a balance to be kept. We may listen to too many Christians, all saying different things, and become terribly confused. But at least we should be sure that we are genuinely 'open to reason'. If God spoke to Balaam through an ass, he can certainly speak through the most mulish member of a Christian fellowship!

Thirdly, God guides us through *his word*. 'Thy word is a lamp to my feet and a light to my path' (Psalm 119: 105). Exactly how we use the Bible for guidance is a very important matter. To open the book at random and pick out the first text that seems relevant, is, of course, a dangerous practice. The Bible is not a talisman or ouija board with mysterious spiritual powers. Texts out of context can say anything and prove nothing. Examples no doubt can be found where a random text proved to be God's leading to someone seeking to know his will; but the exception never proves the rule. Rather, as Paul puts it, 'let the word of Christ dwell in you richly, as you teach and admonish one another in all wisdom' (Colossians 3 : 16). The more the word of Christ dwells in us richly, the more we shall understand the mind of Christ on any issue; and we should also then expect the Holy Spirit to bring into our remembrance such passages and verses that are relevant to the question at hand. No doubt, too, verses may leap out at us 'like a lion from a thicket', as Spurgeon once described this, during our ordinary reading and studying of the Bible. These verses should be noted carefully, although in themselves they will seldom constitute clear guidance without further confirmation.

Fourthly, God guides us *in prayer*. 'Let the peace of Christ rule [i.e. be the arbiter] in your hearts' (Colossians 3: 15). Never go forward without a sense of God's peace about that matter. This deep, inner conviction, coupled with the other strands already mentioned, is the most vital factor in guidance. We should look at the circumstances, listen to other Christians, watch for verses or passages that 'speak' to us in a personal way; but above all pray for that peace of Christ to settle the issue in our hearts. For this, we need to be still before God. We need to wait for a conscious realisation of his presence. Most difficult of all, we need to listen to him, and wait for him to speak. Usually it is helpful first to spend time in praise and worship, resting quietly in the assurance of his love. Guidance becomes virtually impossible when we are in a hurry, except in special circumstances. God never bows to our haste. Therefore we need to focus our whole attention upon him before we can expect that inner conviction and peace. In the Acts 13 passage, which we have already discussed, it was while they were worshipping the Lord and fasting that the Spirit was able to speak. Further, our whole relationship with God is a crucial factor in guidance. Jesus knew his Father's will at every step because, as he was able to say, 'I always do what is pleasing to him' (John 8: 29). It is no good expecting clear guidance unless we are seeking all the time to maintain a close relationship with God. Spending time with him simply to obtain guidance is not enough; we must learn constantly to abide in his love.

These four strands are not the only ways in which God can lead us. Being an infinite God, he has immensely varied forms of communication. 'When [Paul] had seen the vision, immediately we sought to go into Macedonia, concluding that God had called us to preach the gospel to them' (Acts 16: 10). We read in the New Testament of dreams, visions, angels, prophecies, words of knowledge and wisdom, revelations, casting lots (which significantly appears to have ceased after the coming of the Spirit at Pentecost), prayer and fasting—all these and more formed a vital part in the guidance of the Holy Spirit in different places and situations. It would, of course, be unwise to develop an unhealthy dependence on dreams and visions when much more ordinary means of guidance are unquestionably the norm, but we must not limit God to the norm on every occasion. As in most aspects of the Christian life, the temptation is to swing to one extreme or to the other; whereas Scripture is always

beautifully balanced. We should aim to become naturally supernatural and supernaturally natural!

THE TRANSFORMATION OF THE CHRISTIAN

'The fruit of the Spirit is love, joy, peace, patience,
kindness, goodness, faithfulness, gentleness, self-
control' (Galatians 5: 22–23). Notice carefully that
these qualities are essentially not human but divine:
a product of the direct working on the human personality by the Spirit of God. No doubt, however,
there are a great number of complete unbelievers who
demonstrate love, joy and peace. What is the difference? Where is the distinction between believer and
unbeliever?

The answer is twofold. In the first place there should
be a quality of love (the same argument applies to the
rest of the fruit of the Spirit) which is not possible, or
at least not natural, in the ordinary person. As Paul
comments, 'Why, one will hardly die for a righteous
man—though perhaps for a good man one will dare
even to die. But God shows his love for us in that while
we were yet sinners Christ died for us' (Romans 5:
7–8). It is this love that caused Jesus to pray even for
his murderers, and Stephen for his—*that* is the fruit
of the Spirit. It is the love that loves the unlovely, that
forgives seventy times seven, that 'is patient and kind
... not jealous or boastful ...'; the love that 'bears all
things, believes all things, hopes all things, endures all
things'—*that* love is the fruit of the Spirit.

Indeed the same could be said of all the qualities
that Paul lists in Ephesians 5. James tells his readers
to 'count it all joy ... when you meet various trials';

Peter says that Christians in testing situations can still, through believing in Christ, 'rejoice with unutterable and exalted joy'. Jesus said 'Blessed are you when men revile you and persecute you ... rejoice in that day, and leap for joy ...' Christians who have suffered intensely for their faith have frequently experienced this supernatural joy welling up inside them. 'Alone in my cell,' wrote Richard Wurmbrand,[1] 'cold, hungry, and in rags, I danced for joy every night ... Sometimes I was so filled with joy that I felt I would burst if I did not give it expression.' Whether in these or in less testing circumstances, Christians down the centuries have found that Jesus does indeed give his promised fullness of joy and that no one can take that joy from them.

So it is with all the fruit of the Spirit. We can know 'the peace of God, which passes all understanding', a patience which reflects the astonishing patience of God's grace when faced with our arrogant stubbornness—these are all supernatural qualities which transcend our ordinary, natural inclinations towards people and situations.

There is, however, a second basic distinction between the Christian and non-Christian. It is not enough to be loving and kind. Almost anyone can be that. The Christian must bring God to others – must reveal the fragrance of Christ. Duncan Campbell, who brought with him a sense of the presence of God as much as anyone I ever met, once wrote: 'The greatest thing about us all is not what we say, it is not what we do; the greatest thing about us all is our unconscious influence, and that unconscious influence impregnated

[1] *In God's Underground*, Hodder and Stoughton.

by the life of Jesus.' Indeed there is no greater evidence of the presence and power of the Spirit than someone's life and character being steadily transformed into the beauty of Christ. And only the Spirit of God can do that. Whatever else we may look for of the Spirit's work in the individual, nothing could be more important, or more wonderful, than the fruit of love, joy, peace and all the other qualities that can change any person into the likeness of God's own Son.

How does this happen? The New Testament makes it clear that, while it is only the Spirit who can thus transform our lives, we are not to sit back, wrongly assuming that it is all his work and not ours. Always there is a divine-human co-operation: 'Work out your own salvation with fear and trembling; for God is at work in you, both to will and to work for his good pleasure' (Philippians 2: 12f.). It is not enough 'to let go and to let God'. 'No!' says Paul. '*You* work and *God* will work.' And the Scriptures are full of injunctions to 'resist the devil', to 'stand fast', to 'fight the good fight', to 'run that you may obtain', to 'touch nothing unclean', to 'put to death what is earthly in you', to 'put on love'. If God is to work within us, we on our part must be prepared for personal discipline, regular prayer, constant study of the Scriptures and spiritual warfare. Vigorous effort is called for, on the part of the individual Christian. However, and this is the point to be stressed, such discipline, prayer, Bible study and warfare must be in the strength of the Spirit, not in the energy of the flesh. 'If *by the Spirit* you put to death the deeds of the body you will live' (Romans 8: 13); 'Walk *by the Spirit*, and do not gratify the desires of the flesh' (Galatians 5: 16); 'Be strong *in the*

Lord and in the strength of his might' (Ephesians 6: 10); and Paul further explains that righteousness and peace and joy come *'in the Holy Spirit'* (Romans 14: 17).

Perhaps the clearest statement of our determined effort in the power of the Spirit comes at the end of Colossians 1. Here Paul is describing his God-given ministry among the Gentiles. His message had been 'Christ in you, the hope of glory. Him we proclaim, warning every man and teaching every man in all wisdom, that we may present every man mature in Christ.' Then Paul adds this very significant comment: 'For this I toil, striving with all the energy which he mightily inspires within me' (verses 27–29). God expects us to toil and strive with all the strength that we have (or that has been given to us); but all along the way it is the Spirit of God who changes us into his likeness, from one degree of glory to another.

CHAPTER 3

THE HOLY SPIRIT IN THE CHURCH

In the first chapter we noticed the remarkable growth of Pentecostalism in recent years, cutting across not only denominations but also churchmanship and theological backgrounds. Professor F. D. Bruner[1] has called it 'the major religious revolution of our time'. More and more churches, ministers, missionaries, Christians of varying degrees of maturity, are testifying to some charismatic experience. Whatever view we may hold about this, it is impossible to ignore it, and foolish to imagine that it will quickly vanish away. Quite the reverse seems to be true at the moment.

At the centre of the controversy surrounding this aspect of the Spirit's work lies a debate about the 'baptism of the Spirit' and the 'gifts of the Spirit'. We must look at both of these in turn, and see also what it means to be filled with the Spirit.

THE BAPTISM OF THE SPIRIT

Probably more has been written and spoken about this phrase recently than about any other phrase in the whole Bible.

[1] Author of *A Theology of the Holy Spirit*, Hodder and Stoughton.

Is every believer baptised in the Spirit? Does it happen automatically at regeneration? Is it a universal blessing for all members of the new covenant because it is an initial blessing? Or, is it always separate and distinct from the initial conversion experience? Indeed, does it describe primarily an experience or a status? To quote two famous Christian leaders and Biblical expositors.

(a) 'According to Scripture, we have been baptised with the Spirit because we have repented and believed ... I would appeal to you not to urge upon people a baptism with the Spirit as a second and subsequent experience entirely distinct from conversion, for this cannot be proved from Scripture.'[2]

(b) 'I am convinced that there are large numbers of Christian people who are quenching the Spirit unconsciously by denying these possibilities in their very understanding of the doctrine of the Spirit. There is nothing, I am convinced, that so quenches the Spirit as the teaching which identifies the baptism of the Holy Ghost with regeneration.'[3]

Clearly, these two quotations represent widely differing views; and in the debate in the Church as a whole, not all the discussion has been in love, and feelings one way or another still run high. The aim of this brief study of the phrase is not to claim that this is 'the truth' and that nothing more need be said (how arro-

[2] *The Baptism and Fullness of the Holy Spirit*, by John R. W. Stott, I.V.P., pp. 27, 39.

[3] 'Quenching the Spirit', a sermon by Dr. D. Martyn Lloyd-Jones, *The Westminster Record*, September 1964, p. 135.

gant we can be!); but to state a number of proposi-
tions, which, it is hoped, will lead to further prayerful
and humble study.

*First Proposition: All Christians are agreed that every
Christian has the Holy Spirit.* 'Anyone who does not
have the Spirit of Christ does not belong to him'
(Romans 8: 9). And any attempt to drive a wedge between the Spirit of Christ and the Spirit of God is to
plunge straight into dangerous heresy.

*Second Proposition: All Christians are agreed that not
every Christian is filled with the Spirit.* After all, we
may grieve or quench the Spirit; and the command
'Be filled with the Spirit' is a present imperative: 'go
on and on being filled' is the force of it.

*Third Proposition: Not all Christians are agreed about
the phrase 'the baptism of the Spirit'.* The argument
has normally ranged over certain passages in the Acts
of the Apostles (1: 5; 2: 4, 38; 8: 14–17; 9: 17; 10:
44–48; 11: 15–16; 19: 1–6), three parallel passages in
the gospels (Matthew 3:11; Mark 1: 8; Luke 3: 16),
John 1:33 and 1 Corinthians 12: 13. Whatever view is
'the right one', at the very least a good case can be
made out for either position.

*Fourth Proposition: The term 'baptism' is un-
doubtedly linked with Christian initiation*; and in that
sense, at least, every Christian is already baptised in
the Spirit. It is not a question of haves and have-nots.
'Blessed be the God and Father of our Lord Jesus
Christ, who has blessed us in Christ with every

spiritual blessing in the heavenly places' (Ephesians 1 : 3). Once we are in Christ, we have everything—potentially at least.

Fifth Proposition: The term 'baptism' or 'baptise' is a rich word, and in secular literature it meant 'plunge, sink, drown, drench, overwhelm'. A person could be overwhelmed (lit. baptised) by debts, sorrow, calamity; or overcome (lit. baptised) by wine or sleep. Euripedes in the Orestes uses *bapto* when water is splashing into a ship, but *baptizo* when the ship is waterlogged or sinks. In the Old Testament the word again means 'overwhelm, immerse'. 'My mind reels' says Isaiah in 21 : 4—literally he is saying 'the mind is baptised' or overwhelmed. In 2 Kings 5 : 14 Naaman 'dipped [lit. baptised] himself seven times in the Jordan'—this was clearly to all intents and purposes an immersion! In the New Testament, we have the same thought following through. Christ thinking of his coming sufferings on the Cross, talks of 'the baptism with which I am baptised' (Mark 10 : 38f.), speaking of his overwhelming suffering soon to come. Further, the promised baptism of the Spirit at Pentecost resulted in an overwhelming of the Spirit, an overwhelming of the love and power of God which so thoroughly transformed the timid disciples that on and on they went, rejoicing, praising, witnessing—the love of Christ constraining them. Nothing could stop them, not just because of the theological fact of their Christian initiation; but because of the overwhelming of the Spirit in terms of their personal experience. Obviously care must be taken not to press too precisely the nature of the experience (this no doubt varied from person to person), but we must not be frightened of experience. How can you have a vital relationship with the living Lord Jesus without some experience? How can you be filled with the mighty Spirit of God without some experience? How can you worship God in spirit and truth without some experience? Certainly we must beware of seeking experiences just for their own sake, but the New Testament portrait of the Christian is full of superlatives: the peace which passes understanding, the love which surpasses knowledge, unutterable and exalted joy. Jesus said to his disciples that he had spoken these things to them 'that my joy may be in you, and that your joy may be full' (John 15: 11). The Bible is shot through with an atmosphere of praise and rejoicing. Suffering, conviction of sin, chastening, humbling, persecution—yes. But, with repentance for sin, faith in Jesus Christ and the fullness of the Holy Spirit, the New Testament Christian should know a quality of love and joy, life and peace that the world can neither give nor take away.

Sixth Proposition: 'Baptised' speaks both of 'initiated into' and of 'overwhelmed by'—the one a status, the other an experience. Confusion arises when either is stressed at the expense of the other. For example, it is possible to think of the overwhelming of the Spirit as something entirely separate from Christian initiation, whereas the two, ideally and potentially, though not necessarily experientially are one. On the other hand, it is possible so to stress that the Christian has 'got it all' by being baptised into Christ, that the overwhelming of the Spirit is never experienced. For those who make the latter mistake, Dr. Martyn Lloyd-Jones rightly asks, 'Got it all? Well, if you have "got it all" I simply ask, in the name of God, why are you as you are? If you have got it all, why are you so unlike the New Testament Christians? Got it all! Got it at your conversion! Well, where is it, I ask?'[4]

Seventh Proposition: In the last analysis it is the love and power and reality of the Spirit that counts, not the phrase. I am not saying that we should be careless in our use of Biblical words and phrases—far from it! But it is the greatest mistake to argue and fight over terminology of clearly secondary importance, for, whether we are right or wrong, the Spirit will certainly in that case be grieved by our whole attitude (Ephesians 5: 30–32). We may easily have the right phrase but the wrong spirit, and the Holy Spirit is then quite unable to work through us as he wills. The whole purpose of the Spirit's fullness and power is that we should be bold and effective witnesses for Jesus. And it is out of the abundance of the heart that the mouth will speak. If I carry a full glass, and I am jogged and jolted, what will spill out? Whatever is in it, of course. As we are jogged and jolted in our daily life, as we are given opportunities to witness for Christ, what will 'spill out' of our mouth? Whatever is filling our heart! And if our heart is full of the Spirit, filled with the love of Jesus, we are bound to witness naturally and spontaneously to Jesus. The tragedy is, that Christians often do not bear witness, because they have no witness to bear. Dutifully, perhaps, we trot out gospel phrases and doctrinal statements; but others

[4] 'Quenching the Spirit', *The Westminster Record*, September 1964.

fail to see Jesus, they cannot hear Jesus, they do not meet with Jesus. And in that situation, what right have we to be arguing over fruitless terminology?

THE FULLNESS OF THE SPIRIT

We are safe only when the love of God is shed abroad in our hearts by the Holy Ghost, only when our intellects are indwelt by the loving Fire that came at Pentecost. For the Holy Spirit is not a luxury, not something added now and again to produce a de luxe type of Christian once in a generation. No, he is for every child of God a vital necessity, and that he fill and indwell his people is more than a languid hope. It is rather an inescapable imperative![5]

How, then, can a Christian be filled with the Spirit? The answer can be summarised in four words: Repent, Obey, Thirst, Ask.

Repent
Peter preached to the Jerusalem crowd on the day of Pentecost: 'Repent ... and you shall receive the gift of the Holy Spirit' (Acts 2: 38). There are no short cuts or easy terms. We must mean business with God before God will do business with us. There must therefore be a clear, ruthless break with all known sin, plus a determination to put right, with the help of Jesus, all that has been wrong in our life; wrong attitudes, wrong relationships, wrong priorities, wrong use of

[5] *The Divine Conquest*, by A. W. Tozer; Oliphants, 1964, p. 103.

time and money, wrong ambition. All self-sins in our life must go. No compromise is allowed.

Obey

'We are witnesses to these things,' said Peter, 'and so is the Holy Spirit whom God has given to those who obey him' (Acts 5: 32). The immediate context of this verse is obedience in witnessing to Jesus. When the apostles were told not to teach in the name of Jesus, Peter with the others immediately replied, 'We must obey God rather than men', for God gives the Holy Spirit to those who obey him. We must therefore be willing for God to do what he likes with us, to use us as he wants, to send us where he chooses, to make us what he has planned for us to be. Unless I really desire to glorify God in my life, at whatever cost and in whatever way, I do not want to be filled with the Spirit. I may want comforting experiences, but I do not long for the Spirit of God to possess and control my life.

Thirst

'Blessed are those who hunger and thirst for righteousness, for they shall be satisfied [or filled],' said Jesus in the fourth Beatitude. And the first three Beatitudes make it clear what will lead to such a hunger and thirst. First there is a realisation of my own utter spiritual poverty in the sight of God; secondly a profound sorrow concerning my spiritual state; thirdly a humble spirit which says to God 'Not my will but thine be done'; and then comes this great longing to be right with God, filled with his love and power. Such a person will be 'blessed' and 'satisfied', said Jesus.

One of the clearest passages on this is Luke 11 : 1-13. In verse 1 we are told Jesus was talking with his disciples; and certainly a true, personal knowledge of Jesus is essential before there can be any fullness of the Spirit—although in fact both could begin at the same time. In verses 5-8, Jesus went on to tell that delightful story of a man who is embarrassed by a hungry visitor at midnight. The man welcomes him, but promptly goes to his neighbour, banging loudly on his door and saying, 'A friend of mine has arrived on a journey, *and I have nothing to set before him.*' Now that is the context of the promise of the Spirit. When we are sufficiently aware of our own personal need, when we realise that spiritually we have nothing whatever to offer hungry people around us who are coming to us for help, then Jesus encourages us with the assurance of the Spirit's power.

He then anticipated two very common stumbling-blocks. The first is *unbelief*: 'This will not happen to me now.' Therefore he said, underlining it six times, 'And I tell you, Ask, and it will be given you; seek and you will find; knock and it will be opened to you. For everyone who asks receives, and he who seeks finds, and to him who knocks it will be opened.' It *will* happen! And the second difficulty is *fear*: 'What will God do with me? What will happen if nothing happens? Supposing I should experience something spurious or even devilish? What if . . .? Jesus went on: 'What father among you, if his son asks for a fish, will instead of a fish give him a serpent; or if he asks for an egg, will give him a scorpion?' Don't be afraid! God will not trick you, deceive you or hurt you! He will not allow you to be ensnared by evil spirits. Providing you come to the heavenly Father with the one desire to glorify his name, you have nothing to fear. 'If you then, who are evil, know how to give good gifts to your children, how much more will your heavenly Father give the Holy Spirit to those who ask him!'

The nature of faith is to take a promise of God, believe it to be true, claim it humbly yet confidently, and then start praising God that *it is already true*, whether or not the experience of its truth comes immediately. When Mary received the promise of the angel about the coming birth of a Son, she started praising God for what had, in one sense, already happened: 'He who is mighty has done great things for me' (Luke 1 : 49). It was a pure statement of faith. But in fact her Son was not only born; he later went on to teach, 'Whatever you ask in prayer, believe that you receive it [or, have received it'—*N.E.B.*], and you will' (Mark 11 : 24).

Never worry unduly about the precise nature of the experience. Leave that to God. Some experiences of the Spirit's fullness may seem sudden and dramatic; others gradual and gentle. The important thing is to believe that God means what he says. Go out trusting in the Holy Spirit to use you to glorify Jesus. Go on day by day being filled with the Spirit. Watch out for the spiritual battle, which may well be more real than ever. Use the promised power especially to witness to Jesus.

THE GIFTS OF THE SPIRIT

The classic section in the New Testament on this subject is 1 Corinthians 12–14. These chapters are like a honey sandwich, with love as the honey in the middle. Unfortunately, some lick the honey and ignore the rest of the sandwich, which is missing the whole point of chapter 13; while others swallow the bread but forget about the honey, and that is bad for the spiritual digestion! It is therefore important to stress the 'both/and' aspect of these chapters.

After a series of rhetorical questions at the end of chapter 12, implying that different gifts are for different members of the body of Christ, Paul goes on to say, 'But earnestly desire the higher gifts. And I will show you a still more excellent way . . .' (verse 31). Some have interpreted 'higher gifts' as meaning love. But Paul says 'gifts' in the plural, and anyway nowhere in the New Testament is love described as a gift. It is part of the fruit of the Spirit, but not strictly speaking a gift. Therefore, the 'higher gifts' surely refer to the gifts of the Spirit which build up the body of Christ. In 1 Corinthians 14: 12 Paul writes, 'Since you are eager for the manifestations of the Spirit, strive to excel in building up the Church.' Thus when Paul says that he wants to show the Corinthian Christians 'a still more excellent way' he means, in the context, a still more excellent way of manifesting the gifts of the Spirit—namely, in the atmosphere of love. He further summarises this conclusion in the first verse of chapter 14: 'Make love your aim, and earnestly desire the spiritual gifts . . .' Not *either* love *or* gifts; but *both/and*. The gifts of the Spirit are essentially gifts of compassion; expressions of the love of Christ to strengthen the body of Christ. If used as a display of spiritual experience they are, of course, misused; and the Christians concerned are guilty of being carnal and divisive. Love should therefore not only express itself in gifts, it should also be the controlling factor of the gifts—the 'still more excellent way'.

It is worth noticing also that, after his fairly lengthy treatment of this subject, Paul goes on to remind the Corinthians of the essential message of salvation (1 Corinthians 15: 1–4). Of first and foremost importance is the death of Christ for our sins and his glorious resurrection. It is only by this gospel that we can be saved. The balance here is so important. The devil is always trying to lead us off from our main task. If he can make the gifts of the Spirit the central theme in someone's message and ministry, he has won a strategic battle. 'Christ crucified and risen'—this is God's power for salvation.

Before we look at the spiritual gifts in more detail, it is important to notice carefully the safeguards that Paul gives in the first three verses of 1 Corinthians 12: 'Now concerning spiritual gifts, brethren, I do not want you to be uninformed. You know that when you were heathen, you were led astray to dumb idols, however you may have been moved. Therefore I want you to understand that no one speaking by the Spirit of God ever says "Jesus be cursed!" and no one can say "Jesus is Lord" except by the Holy Spirit.'

This is a small but highly significant paragraph. How can we test whether some spiritual experience is true or false, genuine or counterfeit, divine or satanic? There were false prophets and deceiving spirits in the first century, not least at Corinth, and today we face exactly the same dangers. Paul gives two helpful tests.

First, there is the *nature of the gift itself*. The key

words in verses 2 and 3 are 'moved' and 'speaking'. 'Moved' suggests lack of control, or irresistibly drawn; whereas 'speaking' implies full control. This is an important distinction to make. One mark of satanic activity is that of compulsive behaviour; a person is liable to be taken over by an evil spirit, and subject to experiences (often harmful and disturbing) altogether outside his or her control. In most forms of spiritism, for example, an attempt to manipulate supernatural powers for one purpose or another frequently leads to being manipulated by them. The individual is 'irresistibly drawn' to act or think in a compulsive way. However, the Holy Spirit of God is utterly different. He never forces or compels; he never violates the human personality. Certainly there may be divine pressure on us at times—promptings, conviction, guidance and so forth. But always God wants us, by his Spirit, to be glad and willing 'workers together with Christ'. Translations which call speaking in tongues 'ecstatic utterance' or 'ecstatic language' (*The New English Bible*, for example) are thoroughly misleading. Although ecstasy includes the idea of an exalted state of feeling and delight, it very much suggests an altogether uncontrolled state of mind and emotion, which is not true when the Holy Spirit is present. He works graciously and gently within us, since his primary concern is not to produce spiritual excitement, but to glorify Christ.

The second test, given by Paul, concerns the *Lordship of Christ*. 'Therefore I want you to understand that no one speaking by the Spirit of God ever says "Jesus be cursed!" and no one can say "Jesus is Lord" except by the Holy Spirit' (verse 3). This probably referred to a particular doctrinal problem within the Corinthian situation. But a good, practical test for the validity of the Spirit's work is this: what place has Jesus Christ in that Christian or in that Church? When the Spirit comes, said Jesus, 'he will bear witness to me', 'he will glorify me.' Therefore, in practice, a genuine work of the Spirit should result in a greater love for Jesus and a greater obedience to Jesus. 'Jesus is Lord' is not simply a formula. It should be a fact in the life of any fellowship or individual Christian if the Holy Spirit is really active.

Turning to the gifts themselves, Paul summarises his teaching in four phrases in verses 4–7.

'Varieties of gifts' (verse 4)

The Greek word for gifts is *charismata* (hence the 'charismatic' work of the Spirit). The singular, *charisma*, denotes any gift freely and graciously given, and in secular literature was sometimes used of a birthday present. It is essentially a gift of love—or, in the New Testament, a gift of God's love. Therefore we should never be nervous or frightened of these gifts, for they are primarily demonstrations of the love of God for the benefit of others within the body of Christ. Often we may be faced with deep and difficult problems when we do not know what to do, or have no power to do it. Here we need the love and compassion of Jesus, expressed in a gift of his grace suitable for that particular problem. Notice that these gifts are so important that the whole Trinity is involved. Paul mentions 'the same Spirit' (verse 4), 'the same Lord' (verse 5) and 'the same God' (verse 6).

Therefore these gifts are not to be ignored or neglected. Notice, too, that there is a great variety of gifts. In verses 8–10 we have nine of the more remarkable ones; verses 28–30 add apostles, teachers, helpers, administrators; Ephesians 4: 11 includes evangelists and pastors; and Romans 12 speaks about serving, exhorting, giving (money and aid) and 'acts of mercy'. Thus, depending on how we group these gifts, there are either seventeen, nineteen or twenty-one distinct gifts (commentaries differ about this) that are mentioned in the Scriptures, most of which are unquestionably for use today. It therefore seems purely arbitrary to say that some gifts (such as tongues and prophecy) have once-and-for-all disappeared. Where is the Scriptural support for this? Why is there such detailed teaching about the use of tongues and prophecy in 1 Corinthians 14, if this is purely of historical interest? What about the claimed experience of many millions of Christians today, unless we dare to judge that it is all spurious or counterfeit? Some would quote 1 Corinthians 13: 8–12 to indicate that these more unusual gifts were given only until the completion of the New Testament. But has knowledge passed away? Has the perfect come? Do we now see face to face? Do we now understand fully? The present debate over the work of the Holy Spirit (quite apart from many other doctrinal issues) makes it very clear that 'now I know in part' and 'our knowledge is imperfect'. However, lest some gifts should be given undue prominence, it is important to remember that even 'helpers' and 'administrators' are gifts given by God's Spirit. These too need a dependence on, and the guidance of, the Holy Spirit for an effective, spiritual contribution to

79

the whole body of Christ. (Secretaries, treasurers and committee members, please note!)

'Varieties of service' (verse 5)

The word *diakoniai* suggests 'an eager readiness to serve', the root being *eukoneo* which means to hurry or to be in haste. Thus, the gifts of the Spirit will never be forced on an unwilling Christian, but are waiting to be given to those willing to be used. True, 'the Spirit apportions to each one individually as he wills' (verse 11); yet Paul says that we must 'earnestly desire the spiritual gifts'. In most cases we must seek if we are to find; if we do not seek we will not find. God frequently withholds his gifts until he sees that we are ready for them and genuinely wanting them for his glory alone. Of course, a wise balance is called for here, as is so often the case. It is possible to be trapped into the snare of seeking after certain gifts in such a way that is out of all proportion to the rest of our Christian experience, especially perhaps over the matter of tongues. This has the multiple danger of leading to depression if the gift is not given, deception if a counterfeit is experienced, or spiritual pride if the search is rewarded. On the other hand we *are* told earnestly to desire the gifts that will edify the body of Christ; and remembering that these gifts include teaching and evangelism as well as tongues and prophecy, it is important that this 'seeking for the gifts' is not despised when the motives are right.

'Varieties of working' (verse 6)

The word is *energemata*, from which we derive our word energy. It is essentially an active, dynamic word.

suggesting divine energy flowing through someone. Most gifts, therefore, are not a static, permanent possession, but are given as an expression of God's present activity when the need arises. When that happens, Jesus by his Spirit works through his body to bring his help or healing to someone in need. If I then ignore these gifts, or reject them, I could well be guilty of quenching the Spirit and thus preventing the divine energy flowing through me. The fellowship will then not be strengthened or edified in the way that God intends. It is important always to stress that these spiritual gifts are not primarily for personal blessings, but for the whole body of Christ.

However, it also follows from this that special and separate groups, within a church or fellowship, meeting regularly for the purpose of exercising the more unusual gifts, can be divisive and dangerous. It inevitably gives the impression of a spiritual élite, with all the enormous dangers of creating an ungodly distinction between first-class and second-class Christians. Further, this is an entirely false distinction to make, for it in no way follows that the more unusual gifts are the more important ones. However beautiful and meaningful the gift of tongues may be for the believer, is it really more important than the gift of teaching, or of evangelism, or of pastoral help? Moreover, the whole purpose of 1 Corinthians 12 is the essential way in which we belong to one another within the body of Christ. Regardless of the 'importance' of any function, no member can say of another 'I have no need of you.' On the contrary, says Paul, 'The parts of the body which seem to be weaker are indispensable ... But God has so adjusted the body, giving the greater honour to the inferior part, that there may be no discord in the body, but that the members have the same care for one another.' The only grading we are allowed to make is that we are earnestly to desire 'the higher gifts' (the ones which most edify the Church—see 14: 5, 12—whether or not these are the more spectacular gifts), and then to think 'of others as better than ourselves'. After all, whatever blessings we may or may not have had, we are still members of the *one* body of Christ (if we have any personal relationship with him at all); and in every fellowship we all need each other, whatever experiences we may or may not have known.

Further, if any Christians feel frustrated by the lack of spiritual 'freedom' in their situation, or, alternatively. irritated by the 'immaturity' of those who claim some spiritual blessing; what did Jesus feel like during his thirty years in the synagogue at Nazareth, and during his three years with his up-and-down disciples? We must discover a spiritual freedom and maturity in ourselves, or better, in Jesus Christ, not just in our situation.

Also, for those in a Christian Union, or in a Young People's Fellowship, remember that such a grouping is not a local church. There must, in that case, be some limitations, of course. When there is mature, wise, and continuing Christian leadership, coupled with thorough Biblical teaching, and held together by the all-important factor of love, then the more unusual gifts of the Spirit present very few problems. But in certain situations, love will give, for the time being at least, a wise restraint in the exercise of certain gifts. Love never seeks to divide. It is 'eager to maintain the unity of the Spirit in the bond of peace'.

On the other hand, it is clearly unscriptural to forbid certain gifts, such as speaking in tongues (see 1 Corinthians 14: 39 and notice the ringing note of authority in the two verses preceding this), unless the exercise of these gifts becomes disorderly and troublesome. 'All things should be done decently and in order,' concludes the apostle.

'The manifestation of the Spirit' (verse 7)

This verse is perhaps the key to the whole discussion. Almost every word and phrase is instructive. '*To each*' implies on the one hand that the gifts are no guarantee of spiritual maturity. The Corinthian situation makes it clear that while they were 'in every way ... enriched in him ... [and] not lacking in any spiritual gift', they were still 'babes in Christ' and 'as men of the flesh' (see 1 Corinthians 1: 4–7; 3: 1–4). On the other hand, 'to each' implies that the Spirit could give to any Christian one of these gifts, providing they are willing and wanting to be used. Any Christian could therefore be drawn into a vital, spiritual ministry within the body of Christ, and such a ministry does not depend on natural gifts and talents. Indeed, our natural gifts can even be a hindrance to the Spirit until they are seen as worthless without him, for they encourage a self-confidence rather than a Spirit-confidence in Christian work. '*Is given*' (present tense) means 'is continuously being given'. We should expect God to work in this way as part of the normal Christian life. '*The manifestation of the Spirit*'—the Spirit of course is invisible, but he wants to manifest his reality in unmistakable ways. He wants to pull back the veil so that we can see that God is God today. *'For the common good'* (*pros to sympheron*) means 'for the bringing together', for the healing and strengthening of the fellowship. Although I have known sad and tragic abuses of these gifts, I have witnessed on countless occasions the profound strengthening and unifying of the body of Christ when these gifts are rightly manifested in the context of love. As always, the answer to abuse is not disuse but right use.

We must say something about the lesser known and more unusual gifts.

Wisdom describes not so much the natural intelligence of a shrewd Christian, but a word given by God for a specific occasion. To summarise at least part of its meaning:

(*a*) It describes wisdom concerning God. In Isaiah 11 : 2 we have the prophecy that 'the spirit of wisdom and understanding' would rest upon the coming Messiah. And we see the fulfilment of this in the earlier days of Jesus: 'And Jesus increased in wisdom and in stature, and in favour with God and man' (Luke 2 : 52, cf. 2 : 40); whereas later in his ministry we see Jesus with exactly the right word for every situation, often astonishing and silencing his opponents: 'Where did this man get this wisdom?' they all asked (Matthew 13 : 54; cf. Luke 13 : 17; 14 : 6; 20 : 26, 40). Moreover, since Christ has been 'made our wisdom', it is God's plan and purpose that we too should grow in wisdom and be filled with wisdom. The seven deacons were to be men 'full of the Spirit and of wisdom', and Stephen's enemies 'could not with-

stand the wisdom and the Spirit with which he spoke'
(Acts 6 : 3, 10). Further, Paul prayed for the Ephesians
that God might 'give you a spirit of wisdom and of
revelation in the knowledge of him' (Ephesians 1 : 17)
and for the Colossians that they might 'be filled with
the knowledge of his will in all spiritual wisdom and
understanding' (Colossians 1 : 9). Clearly in part, then,
this wisdom refers to a deep understanding of God,
his word and his ways. It applies to those who have
been gifted by God in the interpretation of the Scriptures and the communicating of his truth to others.
This is not dependent on natural scholarship, but
upon a divine gift of wisdom coupled with obedience
to the truth.

(b) Wisdom also describes the God-given ability to
make the right decisions and to say the right words,
often in difficult and testing circumstances. In 1 Kings
3 : 9 King Solomon prayed for such wisdom: 'Give
thy servant therefore an understanding mind to
govern thy people, that I may discern between good
and evil.' God, pleased with this request, at once
promised him 'a wise and discerning mind', which was
immediately tested by two women coming to him
with two babies, one dead and one alive. Each mother
insisted that the living child was her own. Through
a word of wisdom given to Solomon the situation was
quickly resolved! (1 Kings 3 : 16–28). In the New
Testament, Jesus warned his disciples of persecution,
but promised them: 'I will give you a mouth and
wisdom which none of your adversaries will be able to
withstand or contradict' (Luke 21 : 15—a promise not
to be wrenched out of context to support a super-

spiritual, anti-intellectual laziness when it comes to preparing talks and sermons!).

Knowledge refers primarily to a God-given insight into something normally outside our natural understanding.

(*a*) It may refer to our knowledge of God: 'The secret things belong to the Lord our God; but the things that are revealed belong to us' (Deuteronomy 29: 29). When Daniel was asked by King Nebuchadnezzar if he was 'able to make known the dream', he replied, 'There is a God in heaven who reveals mysteries' (Daniel 2: 26–30). Later Paul wrote that the 'depths of God' had been 'revealed to us through the Spirit' (1 Corinthians 2: 10).

(*b*) It may also refer to a special word of knowledge about others. 'How do you know me?' asked Nathanael of Jesus, amazed by his spiritual perception (John 1: 48). Then, in John 4, Jesus revealed to the Samaritan woman that he knew all about her sad and abortive sex life: 'You have had five husbands, and he whom you now have is not your husband.' And the woman at once replied, 'Sir, I perceive that you are a prophet!' (John 4: 17–19). We find this same gift of knowledge in Acts. Peter knew, by the Spirit, all about the false motives in the hearts of Ananias and Sapphira (Acts 5: 1–11); and Paul knew that the cripple at Lystra 'had faith to be made well' (Acts 14: 9)—which led at once to the man's healing. In many situations we need to know the heart of a person's problem; and this is something that God, by his Spirit, may wish to reveal to the counsellor.

Faith. This is not 'saving faith', nor the natural fruit of the Spirit, but a special gift of faith needed for God's work, or in a crisis situation. It is the faith that removes mountains, the faith of those Biblical heroes in Hebrews 11, the faith of Gideon and David, and of course the faith that Jesus revealed in almost every aspect of his life and ministry. When confronted with a rapidly decomposing Lazarus, he said first to Martha, 'Did I not tell you that if you would believe you would see the glory of God?' And then he lifted his eyes to his Father and said, 'Father, I thank thee that thou hast heard me. I know that thou hearest me always, but I have said this on account of the people standing by, that they may believe that thou didst send me.' Then he cried with a loud voice, 'Lazarus, come out' (John 11: 40–43). In the New Testament we see the faith of many individuals: the centurion at Capernaum (Matthew 8: 10), the Canaanite woman (Matthew 15: 22–28), Peter and John at the gate Beautiful (Acts 3: 1–10), Philip obeying the Spirit's guidance (Acts 8) and Paul in his astonishing missionary journeys. In more recent days, George Müller, Hudson Taylor, Brother Andrew, George Verwer, Richard Wurmbrand and many others, have known this gift of faith.

Healing. From the earliest days God has revealed himself as 'I am the Lord, your healer' (Exodus 15: 26). And it is clear that, in God's sovereignty, not only Jews but pagans have experienced the healing power of God (Naaman, for example, in 2 Kings 5). But while there were many sudden and instantaneous healings, King Azariah remained sick until the end of his life, even though 'he did what was right in the eyes of the Lord' (2 Kings 15: 3)—partly, no doubt, because 'the high places [heathen sacrifices] were not taken away'. And Job continued with his very painful disease for a considerable time: James talks of the 'patience of Job'. We need to beware of an over-simplification in the realm of healing—'If you have faith you will be well.' It is not always quite so straight-forward as that.

However, in the New Testament it is clear that the healings of body and mind and the exorcisms of evil spirits were all part of the preaching of the gospel. They were all signs that the Kingdom of God had come. 'And he called to him his twelve disciples and gave them authority over unclean spirits, to cast them out, and to heal every disease and every infirmity ... "And preach as you go, saying 'The kingdom of heaven is at hand.' Heal the sick, raise the dead, cleanse lepers, cast out demons"' (Matthew 10: 1, 7–8). In the early Church the same pattern continued: 'Philip ... proclaimed to them the Christ. And the multitude gave heed to what was said by Philip, when they heard him and saw the signs which he did. For unclean spirits came out of many who were possessed ... and many who were paralysed or lame were healed' (Acts 8: 5–7). Paul also explained that his fruitful evangelistic ministry had been 'by word and deed, by the power of signs and wonders, by the power of the Holy Spirit' (Romans 15: 18f.).

Today, similar evidence may at times accompany

the preaching of the gospel. Supremely we need the evidence of changed lives; but the Church as a whole is rightly rediscovering the healing ministry for body, mind and spirit, through the power of the Spirit of God. Significantly, in 1 Corinthians 12 Paul speaks of gifts (plural) of healing. Each fresh healing is a fresh gift from God. The 'gift of healing' is not owned by a person, but is given to the one who is sick. Therefore, in any healing ministry there must be a complete and constant dependence on God for this power to heal. There is no technique, no formula, no guarantee. All is from God. 'The prayer of faith will save the sick man, and the Lord will raise him up,' says James, giving instructions about the ministry of healing within a local church.

Miracles refer to acts of God wider than healings. In the Old Testament these were common enough at certain periods of Israel's history: the miracles from Egypt to the Promised Land, and of Elijah and Elisha, for example. In the New Testament we have the stilling of the storm, the walking on the water, the feeding of the five thousand; and in John 14: 12 Jesus promised his disciples, 'Truly, truly, I say to you, he who believes in me will also do the works that I do; and greater works than these will he do, because I go to the Father.' At Pentecost, the fulfilment of this promise was obvious. Yet still they prayed that 'signs and wonders' would be performed in the name of Jesus (Acts 4: 30). Prison doors were opened, divine judgments fell, the dead were raised; and so common were 'ordinary miracles' that we are told in Acts 19: 11 that 'God did extraordinary miracles by the hands of

Paul'! Today there are reports of unusual manifestations of God's power all over the world. It is said that in the recent Indonesian revival every New Testament miracle has occurred at least once, sometimes on many occasions.[6]

Prophecy is a message from God, which is not necessarily anything to do with the future: a forth-telling, not primarily a foretelling. All this, of course, was very common in the Old Testament days when God's word normally came through the prophets. Here people were not speaking with their own authority, but were able to proclaim, 'Thus says the Lord'. Sometimes their prophecies were the result of visions and unusual revelations from God. In the New Testament, first John the Baptist, and then Jesus himself, took on this prophetic ministry. Again there were visions and voices, but always this note of authority: 'The crowds were astonished at his teaching, for he taught them as one who had authority, and not as their scribes' (Matthew 7: 28f.). In the New Testament Church, the gift of prophecy continued with the coming of the Spirit: 'This is what was spoken by the prophet Joel: "And in the last days it shall be, God declares, that I will pour out my Spirit upon all flesh, and your sons and your daughters shall prophesy, and your young men shall see visions, and your old men shall dream dreams; yea, and on my menservants and my maidservants in those days I will pour out my Spirit; and they shall prophesy" ' (Acts 2: 16–18). This quotation from Joel

[6] See, for example, *The Revival in Indonesia* by Dr. Kurt E. Koch, Evangelization Publishers; *Miracles in Indonesia* by Don Crawford, Tynedale Publishers, 1972.

is of particular importance. Most commentators agree that 'the last days' refer to the period between Christ's first and second coming; therefore this gift of prophecy is to continue until Christ's return (cf. 1 Corinthians 13: 8–10). Further, anyone might be given a gift of prophecy—women as well as men. As it seems clear that, in the early Church at least, there were no women preachers (1 Corinthians 14: 33–36; 1 Timothy 2: 11–15), prophecy and preaching were not the same thing, even if there might be an overlap on occasions. Philip's four daughters all prophesied, and it is almost inconceivable that they were preachers in that first-century Church. Further, Paul said to the Corinthians: 'You can all prophesy one by one, so that all may learn and all be encouraged (1 Corinthians 14: 31). What is prophecy, then? Paul gives the answer to this in verse 3 of that chapter: 'He who prophesies speaks to men for their upbuilding and encouragement and con-solation.' It is a word from the Lord through a mem-ber of the body of Christ, inspired by the Spirit, to build up the rest of the body (1 Corinthians 14: 3–5). Nor was prophecy just for the completion of the canonical scriptures. Obviously there were numerous prophecies unrecorded, but they fulfilled their im-mediate task of strengthening the spiritual life of the local congregation. This ministry is tremendously im-portant for every age, and is not made redundant by the completion of the God-given revelation in the Scriptures.

Discerning of spirits. This is immensely important, as every genuine work of God is challenged and counter-feited by Satan. In Acts 16: 17 Paul and Silas were pestered by a girl who kept on crying out, 'These men are servants of the Most High God, who proclaim to you the way of salvation.' This was quite true. But Paul, through the Spirit's gift of discernment, knew that this girl was speaking by a spirit of divination and therefore a threat to God's work at Philippi. Jesus himself would never tolerate true statements about his person when these came from demons. Therefore Paul said to the spirit, 'I charge you in the name of Jesus to come out of her.' The New Testament makes it clear that false prophets, deceiving spirits and lying signs and wonders may abound when God is manifesting his power. How can we distinguish between the spirits? How can we know what is demonic, psychological, or divine in origin? The tests are clear. (*a*) Is Jesus Lord of that person's life? 'No one can say "Jesus is Lord" except by the Holy Spirit' (1 Corinthians 12: 13). (*b*) Is Jesus Christ acknowledged as Perfect Man and Perfect God? 'By this you know the Spirit of God: every Spirit which confesses that Jesus Christ has come in the flesh is of God' (1 John 4: 2). (*c*) Is there a measure of true godliness and holiness about the person? 'Every sound tree bears good fruit, but the bad tree bears evil fruit ... Thus you will know them by their fruits' (Matthew 7: 15–20; cf. 2 Peter 2). (*d*) Together with these more objective tests, there can be a spiritual ability, given by the Spirit, to distinguish between the spirits. It is this inner discernment that Jesus and the apostles had in many recorded situations in the New Testament. On a more positive note, it is worth remembering that the possibility of a counterfeit exists only with the presence of the genuine. I have witnessed many counterfeit conversions, but I still evangelise. I have seen counterfeit spiritual experiences, but I still 'earnestly desire the spiritual gifts'. We must not be so frightened of counterfeits that we close our hearts to the genuine gifts of God's love.

Tongues. This has been at the centre of the most heated debate concerning spiritual gifts, probably because it is the one gift less easily understood by our natural minds and experience. This in itself should not worry us, of course, because all God's sovereign working in our life is 'supernatural'. However, the gift of tongues at first sight confuses some people, and frightens or disturbs others. For this reason alone we need to look at this gift in a little more detail; and the following references will all be from 1 Corinthians 14, except where otherwise indicated.

'Tongues' simply means languages given by the Holy Spirit—maybe human or angelic languages (see 1 Corinthians 13:1). They are neither gibberish nor 'ecstatic utterances'. They are straightforward languages, with the speaker in full control of the utterance, as in any more usual prayer (see 1 Corinthians 14: 15, 28). Normally the speaker and hearers do not understand the language (verses 2, 14), although there are notable exceptions to this; and therefore there is a need, within a group, for the *gift of interpretation* (verses 13, 27).

It is important to distinguish between the private and public use of tongues. Paul makes this clear in verses 18–19: 'I thank God that I speak in tongues more than you all; nevertheless, in church I would rather speak five words with my mind in order to instruct others, than ten thousand words in a tongue.' Essentially, therefore, tongues is a private, devotional language—a 'love-language' if you like. It is a personal and intimate form of communication between the believer and the Lord (verse 2), when the mind is relaxed, but the spirit is still praising or praying: 'For if I pray in a tongue, my spirit prays but my mind is unfruitful. What am I to do? I will pray with the spirit and I will pray with the mind also: I will sing with the spirit and I will sing with the mind also' (verse 14f.). Some have interpreted this as though Paul wanted always to use the mind at the same time as the spirit; but clearly that is not so from his following statement that he spoke in tongues 'more than you all'. This gift is primarily for spiritual refreshment: 'He who speaks in a tongue edifies himself' (verse 4) —'edify' (*oikodomeo*) meaning build up or strengthen. Further, when using this gift he 'speaks not to men but to God ... he utters mysteries in the Spirit' (verse 2). This gift, therefore, is not irrational (which means unreasonable, illogical, absurd), but supra-rational, something which transcends the ordinary level of rational communication. After all, there are many forms of communication between two people; for example, in prayer, silence or 'sighs too deep for words' (Romans 8: 26) can also be very real and effective. Tongues is simply another expression of our relationship of love with God through Jesus Christ.

Occasionally, according to Paul's instructions, there may be the public use of tongues, but this should happen not more than two or three times at the most in any one meeting, and always there must be an *interpretation*. The primary principle is always the edification of the church: 'He who prophesies is greater than he who speaks in tongues, unless someone interprets, so that the church may be edified' (verse 5). Never should any gift be used as a demonstration of spirituality; always it should be 'for the common good', to strengthen the body of Christ.

Common objections and problems about this gift of tongues are frequently raised, and it is worth looking at these very briefly.

1. 'Tongues were given for preaching in other languages, as in Acts 2. Today missionaries have other ways for learning these languages.'

Answer: The hundred and twenty spoke in tongues, and in so doing were worshipping and praising God ('we hear them telling in our own tongues the mighty works of God'—Acts 2: 11); but only Peter preached. There is no evidence that he spoke in tongues for this, nor that this gift was ever used for preaching the gospel. Clearly there is a uniqueness about the Acts 2 phenomenon. We should expect an unusual manifestation of God's glory accompanying the birth of the Church, just as with the birth of God's Son. It is not every day that the sky is filled with 'a multitude of the heavenly host praising God'; and it is not every day that a hundred and twenty speak in different, recognisable languages at the same time. The coming of the Son of God and of the Spirit of God were both unique and historic occasions. In point of fact, 'tongues' have quite often been languages understood by someone present, but this is not to say that their purpose is for preaching the gospel.

2. 'Tongues are mentioned in detail only in 1 Corinthians. Corinth was a carnal church. This gift, therefore, represents carnal but not spiritual Christianity.'

Answer: The Holy Spirit is the author of all spiritual gifts, including tongues. How could it be 'carnal'? Paul said 'I thank God that I speak in tongues more than you all' (verse 18). It is only we who are carnal in our divisions, rivalry and jealousy. Further, it is worth remembering that detailed teaching about the Lord's Supper is to be found only in this letter to the carnal church at Corinth.

3. 'Paul discouraged its use.'

Answer: He discouraged its misuse, but was always positive about its right use (verses 5, 18, 26, 39).

4. 'It is very emotional, and psychologically dangerous.'

Answer: It need not be 'very emotional' at all. Nevertheless, how genuine is worship, praise and adoration if there is no emotion? It is true that there can be a psychologically induced 'tongue' which is worked up from within; and this could be dangerous. But the gift of the Spirit should bring a psychological release of tensions together with spiritual refreshment.

5. 'It is found in other religions, and therefore could be demonic.'

Answer: We have already seen that Satan counterfeits nearly every genuine work of God. However, God gives us various tests by which to distinguish the true from the false; and we must trust that as we seek for God's gifts in the name of Jesus Christ, he will not allow us to be deceived (see Luke 11 : 11–13).

6. 'It is the least of all the gifts.'

Answer: Certainly it is not at all helpful within a fellowship unless accompanied by interpretation (verses 4–5). However we must be careful about describing (and possibly despising) any gift of the Holy Spirit as 'the least'. This could be dangerously near an affront to God Himself. Every gift of God is good and beautiful, designed for a God-given purpose in our lives.

Paul concludes : 'Make love your aim, and earnestly desire the spiritual gifts, especially that you may prophesy' (1 Corinthians 14 : 1).

THE BODY OF CHRIST

After this brief examination of the nine more unusual spiritual gifts, it may be important to stress again two facts. First, there are many other extremely important gifts within the Church, such as teaching, evangelism, administration and pastoral gifts. Secondly, the whole purpose of 1 Corinthians 12 is not just that we should be informed about these gifts (see verse 1), but also that we should realise a oneness within the body of Christ. 'For just as the body is one and has many members, and all the members of the body are one body, so it is with Christ' (verse 12). Paul is simply saying that we all belong to one another and we all need one another : therefore we should all work together, submitting ourselves to the head of the body, Christ.

In different traditions, the Church for years has been either pulpit-centred or altar-centred. In both situations the dominant rôle has been played by the minister or priest, and all too often they become the bottleneck in their congregation for spiritual growth and activity. In his book *Called to Serve*, Michael Green comments on the spectacular spread of the Pentecostal churches in South America:

> The growth of the Pentecostal churches may be due to many causes, but not least is the fact that it is predominantly a *lay* church. They have, indeed, a ministry, but it is not a hierarchy. The ministers do a secular job, and they really seek to 'equip the saints for the work of service'. As a result every Christian bears constant witness to his faith in impromptu open-air meetings and in personal conversation with his friends. Every Christian is free to participate in the weekly—and nightly—meetings for worship. Doubtless these meetings are often somewhat disorderly, but they are *alive*, because the whole people of God take a real part. He would be a proud man who asserted that we have nothing to learn from them.[7]

As it is by the Spirit that we are baptised into the one body of Christ, it is clearly the Spirit's concern to make us into an effective body, with 'each part working properly'. The early Church worked together, worshipped together, prayed together, studied together, witnessed together, shared together and suffered together. They were as inseparably bound up to each

[7] op. cit., Hodder and Stoughton, 1964, p. 28.

98

other as they were to Christ; and any deviation from this organic structure meant a weakness in the whole system—a diseased body. It is only the Spirit who can fill the body with the love and joy of Jesus Christ. And when this happens, unbelievers may well be impressed by a quality of life, unity and spiritual reality that is outside their natural experience. It is in that situation that they may 'worship God and declare that God is really among you'.

CHAPTER 4

WALKING BY THE SPIRIT

AT the end of the last chapter we saw that to ask God to fill us with the Holy Spirit is not the summit of Christian experience. We have not suddenly arrived! As soon as we begin to know anything of the control of the Spirit, we need at once to learn to walk by the Spirit; and this suggests a steady, continuous way of life: 'If we live by the Spirit, let us also walk by the Spirit' (Galatians 5: 25—the present subjunctive giving the sense, 'let us go on and on walking by the Spirit'). We must learn to fight spiritual battles,[1] and to grow steadily in the knowledge of our Lord Jesus Christ. In particular, we need to realise how vulnerable we still are and how easily we may quench the Spirit in our lives. A greater understanding of this will help us to guard against the most subtle and poisonous sin of all which may often follow a time of personal blessing—personal pride.

QUENCHING THE SPIRIT

What are some of the ways in which we might quench the Spirit, both in our personal lives and in our churches and fellowships?

[1] I have discussed this in some detail in *God's Freedom Fighters*, Movement Books.

By resisting the Spirit's work

'Do not quench the Spirit, do not despise prophesying,' writes Paul (1 Thessalonians 5: 19-20). Most commentators take this to mean that some of the more conservative church members were not too happy about the manifestation of certain gifts of the Spirit, such as prophecy (and perhaps tongues). When writing to the Corinthians, Paul had to discourage the exaggerated display of these gifts; but here it was the more cautious and conservative members who were taking the line that they must avoid extremes at all costs. They therefore tried to stop all manifestations of the more remarkable gifts of the Spirit, for fear of the situation getting out of hand. No doubt they were well-meaning in their caution, but they were in fact quenching the Spirit in the process. It is a profound yet common mistake to have such a tight control on a Christian fellowship that the Holy Spirit is quite unable to move freely 'as he wills'—as *we* will, perhaps, but not as he wills. All too often we have set a premium on tidiness. But in many areas one of the tidiest places you can find is a crematorium. And if it is a choice between tidiness plus death, or some chaos plus life, I know which I would prefer every time, even if life is more demanding and challenging. We must dare to trust God to have his control over his work, for 'unless the Lord builds the house, those who build it labour in vain.'

By going to extremes

In the temptations of Jesus in the wilderness, the devil, having failed with all else, tries to make Jesus superspiritual; 'If you are the Son of God, throw yourself down from here; for it is written, "He will give his angels charge over you, to guard you," and "On their hands they will bear you up, lest you strike your foot against a stone"' (Luke 4: 9–11). Notice that Satan quotes from Scripture to encourage this extravagant and spectacular action. This is a very strong form of temptation for those who really want the best and who are seeking to live by faith. The devil will take what is good, backed often by Biblical promises, and then push it to extremes. For example, guidance by the Spirit is good; but the devil takes it one step further. In a Christian Union why bother about a programme? Why book up speakers? Why not trust the Lord to work it all out? And when it comes to personal matters, why consult other Christians? Why not go ahead as you feel led? And if it does seem a bit unusual, well surely you are stepping out in faith! Again, healing by the Spirit is good. But the devil sees to it that medical help is 'in faith' denied; or that Christians are exorcised of this evil spirit and that evil spirit, when what is probably needed is a straight bit of repentance or obedience! Again, the gifts of the Spirit are good; but Satan tries to make certain that these gifts matter even more than the Giver. In one way or another, the Spirit is quenched.

By bitterness in the fellowship

Paul, writing to the Ephesians, urges them to maintain the unity of the Spirit in the bond of peace. If it is necessary at times to 'speak the truth' it must be done in love so that the whole body can upbuild itself in love. Therefore, he concludes this section of his letter, 'Be angry but do not sin; do not let the sun go down on your anger, and give no opportunity to the devil . . . Let no evil talk come out of your mouths, but only such as is good for edifying, as fits the occasion, that it may impart grace to those who hear. And do not grieve the Holy Spirit of God, in whom you were sealed for the day of redemption. Let all bitterness and wrath and anger and clamour and slander be put away from you, with all malice, and be kind to one another, tenderhearted, forgiving one another, as God in Christ forgave you' (Ephesians 5: 26-32). Grumblings, resentment, criticism, bitterness—they can destroy God's work more quickly than almost anything else. This is one of Satan's commonest and most devastating attacks. 'Strive for peace with all men', says the writer to the Hebrews, 'and for holiness without which no one will see the Lord. See to it that no one fail to obtain the grace of God; that no "root of bitterness" spring up and cause trouble, and by it the many become defiled' (Hebrews 12: 14f.).

Within every fellowship there is the need to love and forgive, to love and forgive, time and time again. Jesus said seventy times seven. Yet, with most of us, resentment and criticism well up when we have been upset only once or twice. If we were upset by a fellow Christian literally no less than four hundred and ninety times, that would take some forgiveness! Yet if the Spirit is not to be quenched, we need to watch our attitudes, our tongues and our relationships very carefully indeed.

By ungodly behaviour

In Ephesians 5, Paul's build-up to his command to be filled with the Spirit is clear and forceful: 'But immorality and all impurity or covetousness must not even be named among you, as is fitting among saints. Let there be no filthiness, nor silly talk, nor levity, which are not fitting. Take no part in the unfruitful works of darkness, but instead expose them. For it is a shame even to speak of the things that they do in secret ... Therefore do not be foolish ... And do not get drunk with wine ...' (Ephesians 5: 3-18). Sin of all kinds will quench or grieve the Spirit immediately. At Corinth, too, there was immense potential. Here God had worked through Paul 'in demonstration of the Spirit and power'; many had a rich and lively experience of spiritual gifts. But the society from which most had been converted was a highly permissive society. Sexual freedom and perversion abounded, and the pressure of this had affected several within the Church. Paul writes vigorously about this, and asks his readers, 'Do you not know that your body is a temple of the Holy Spirit within you, which you have from God? You are not your own; you were bought with a price. So glorify God in your body' (1 Corinthians 6: 19-20). As the love of God is poured into the hearts of Christians by the Holy Spirit, we need to be all the more on our guard lest a genuine, warm, spiritual love degenerates into the love-feasts which became such a scandal at Corinth.

By party spirit

This was another tragic feature of the church at Corinth: the cult of personality—something which afflicts so much of the Church today. Instead of the one, united body of Christ, little groups were following their own little leader: 'I belong to Paul', 'I belong to Apollos', 'I belong to Cephas'. Paul, depressed by this foolish, fleshly, unspiritual rivalry, asks, 'What then is Apollos? What is Paul? Servants through whom you believed, as the Lord assigned to each. I planted, Apollos watered, but God gave the growth. So neither he who plants nor he who waters is anything, but only God who gives the growth ... For we are fellow-workers for God; you are God's field, God's building' (1 Corinthians 3: 5–9). Christians belong to God. They are all part of the body of Christ. Christ is the head of that body. Never should human leadership usurp the place that is God's alone—Father, Son and Holy Spirit. 'My glory I give to no other.' To take from God the honour that is due to his Name alone and to give it to a sinful person (however wise and helpful that person may have become in Christ) is one of the surest ways of quenching the Spirit. Indeed, Paul includes this party spirit as one of the 'works of the flesh' (Galatians: 16–21). And 'the desires of the flesh are against the Spirit', is his clear and solemn warning.

By neglect

In 2 Timothy 1: 6–7 Paul exhorts Timothy 'to re-kindle the gift of God that is within you through the laying on of my hands; for God did not give us a spirit of timidity but a spirit of power and love and self-control'. Here the gift of God is undoubtedly the gift of the Spirit, in his power and fullness. The trouble was that, partly through fear, the fire of the Spirit had died down. It had been neglected and quenched. The Church in general, and individual Christians in particular, urgently need the warmth of God's love, not only filling their own lives, but radiating out to others.

Most people are attracted by warmth; and if our lives and fellowships are cold and loveless, people will go elsewhere for the fire that they need. Emil Brünner once wrote, 'It is because the church has neglected in almost all ages to create a true fellowship in Christ that we are confronted by the phenomenon of modern Communism, which has grown like a wasting disease.' This surely is God's rebuke to a loveless Church. Look at the fire and passion of the early Church: 'Breaking bread in their homes, they partook of food with glad and generous hearts, praising God and having favour with all the people.' And with this wonderful warmth of love and praise, what happened? 'The Lord added to their number day by day those who were being saved' (Acts 2: 46f.). If we neglect the gift of God's Spirit in our lives, if the fire is quenched, there will be a chilling coldness and carelessness which will effectively keep others away from the Saviour we are trying to proclaim. After all, Jesus made it clear that it is 'by this all men know that you are my disciples, if you have love for one another' (John 13: 35).

AGLOW WITH THE SPIRIT

This is the positive side of the same coin. Having seen negatively how we might so easily quench the Spirit, what are some of the ways in which we can obey Paul's command to 'be aglow with the Spirit' (Romans 12: 11)? Let me reduce it to three basic principles as seen in the first-century Church—so obvious and yet so vital.

They were a united fellowship

The early chapters in Acts are liberally sprinkled with phrases indicating their oneness in Christ: 'with one accord', 'all together', 'all things in common', 'of one heart and soul'. God's power is essentially for God's people, and not just for a few individual Christians who happen to be filled with the Spirit. One of the greatest weaknesses of today, especially among evangelicals, is individualism: 'I do my own thing my own way, as I feel led.' However, it is the quality, depth and unity of a Christian fellowship as a whole that is of paramount importance. Christ works through his body. The Spirit apportions gifts to each member as he wills but they are always for the common good. It is 'the whole body, joined and knit together by every joint with which it is supplied, when each part is working properly, [that] makes bodily growth and up-builds itself in love' (Ephesians 4: 16). Moreover, God has promised to command his blessing whenever brothers dwell together in unity (Psalm 133).

Indeed, almost every area of our Christian life can be affected by the degree of unity in the fellowship. To take only one example, prayer: in Matthew 18: 19 Jesus promises his disciples that 'if two of you agree on earth about anything they ask, it will be done for them by my Father in heaven'. The Greek word for agree, *sumphoneo*, means 'in symphony with' or 'in harmony with'. In other words, it is not enough that two or more Christians should mentally assent to the same prayer. Their lives must be in complete harmony with each other. They must be in a relationship of love and forgiveness. If there is any disharmony, bitterness, resentment or jealousy, then at once the power of prayer is broken. There is a most striking example of this in Mark 11. From the remarkable incident of the cursing and withering of the fig-tree, Jesus goes on to teach about the immense power of believing prayer. Even a mountain could be cast into the sea! 'Therefore I tell you, whatever you ask in prayer, believe that you receive it, and you will' (Mark 11 : 24). At that point he adds one more sentence that at first sight seems a curious postscript, quite unrelated to all that has gone before. 'And whenever you stand praying, forgive, if you have anything against anyone; so that your Father also who is in heaven may forgive you your trespasses.' Why is there this sudden exhortation to forgive? It is because that is an essential condition for answered prayer. However often and fervently we may pray, if there is a lack of love and forgiveness, and if there is any disharmony within the fellowship, then frankly, we are wasting our time. All the great revivals and movements of God's Spirit have learnt this same vital lesson. We need to get right, not only with God, but also with one another. It is only when the fellowship is really united and harmonious that we can ever expect any blessing at all.

Over the past ten years or more it has been my privilege to have been involved in many evangelistic missions of one form or another. I know of no other single factor that can so influence a mission, for good or for evil, as this question of relationships between the Christians. Prayer, publicity, imagination, Biblical preaching—all may be present. But the most crucial factor of all is the depth of unity within the body of Christians. Although John 17 has often been mis-quoted and misused to support some rather dubious ecumenical ventures, it is striking to see in this passage Christ's emphasis on this unity between believers. Four times he prays for his disciples 'that they may be one—perfectly one'. Indeed he makes it clear that Christian fellowship should reflect the love and oneness within the Godhead itself. Jesus further goes on to explain why this is so important: 'that the world may believe that thou hast sent me' and 'that the world may know that thou hast sent me'. I will always remember one of the most outstanding and fruitful missions I have ever experienced. Never have I seen such a remarkable response to the gospel of Christ. However, in that church there was an equally remarkable sense of love and oneness among the believers. Over the months and years this had been a most powerful testimony to the whole community of the reality of Christ. No wonder that men and women of all ages and backgrounds flocked into the Kingdom! It is worth adding that the congregation in that church was also very much alive to the Holy Spirit. He is always the one who will give a quality of love that will not naturally be found anywhere else.

They were a praying fellowship

Before Pentecost, the disciples 'all ... with one accord devoted themselves to prayer' (Acts 1: 14). The Spirit of God then fell upon them, and again we see this same emphasis on prayer: 'they devoted themselves to ... the prayers' (2: 42), 'they lifted their voices together to God' (4: 24). The apostles chose seven deacons to carry some of the administrative burdens, because, they explained, 'we will devote ourselves to prayer and to the ministry of the word' (6: 4). Everywhere in the Scriptures you will find this concentration on prayer.

It is interesting, too, to see the place given to worship and praise. Certainly there must be a balance; but praise, more than anything else, will lead to a gracious sense of the presence of God. At the dedication of the temple, in 2 Chronicles 5, when they began unitedly to praise the Lord, 'the glory of the Lord filled the house of God'. In 2 Chronicles 20, God's people were faced with a tremendous battle, 'when they began to sing and praise' God came down in power and gave the victory. The Psalms, of course, are full of praise. Indeed it was when 'our mouth was filled with laughter, and our tongue with shouts of joy, [that] they said among the nations, "The Lord has done great things for them"' (Psalm 126). The New Testament likewise refers frequently to thanksgiving and praise: 'Be filled with the Spirit, addressing one another in psalms and hymns and spiritual songs, singing and making melody to the Lord with all your heart, always and for everything giving thanks in the name of our Lord Jesus Christ to God the Father' (Ephesians 5: 18–20). Moreover, praise is the language of heaven. Read Revelation 4 and 5, 7, 15 and 19. Praise is the language of faith now, but the language of heaven later. In one sense, therefore, it is the meeting-place of heaven and earth; it brings a breath of heaven into our own lives and fellowships. It is possible, of course, to swing to extremes and to neglect other vital forms of prayer: confession of sin and interceding for the needs of others, for example. Praise is no substitute for repentance, and all too often 'we have not because we ask not'. Nevertheless, faith depends directly on our vision of

God. As we therefore begin by praise and worship, our vision of God grows, our faith grows, our expectancy grows, and intercessory prayer becomes very much more powerful. In Acts 4 the disciples were faced with a crisis; the first wave of opposition had broken over the new-born Church. At once they prayed. And in their prayer they spent five verses reminding themselves of the sovereignty of God, and only two verses for their specific request. 'And when they had prayed, the place in which they were gathered was shaken; and they were all filled with the Holy Spirit and spoke the word of God with boldness' (verses 24–31).

In many Christian circles today we have neglected, to our cost, the priority of worship. The Church has two basic functions; first to worship, secondly to witness. It is 'to offer spiritual sacrifices acceptable to God through Jesus Christ' before it declares to others 'the wonderful deeds of him who called you out of darkness into his marvellous light' (1 Peter 2: 5, 9). Unfortunately, worship, for many, has come to mean a few hymns and prayers, arranged in some liturgical or non-liturgical pattern. Whereas 'the true worshipper,' said Jesus, 'will worship the Father in spirit and truth.' Here the combination is important. It is not only a question of *what* we say or sing. It is a question of *how* we say or sing it. It must be from the heart, from our innermost being. Just as the Spirit witnesses with our spirit that we are children of God, prompting us to cry 'Abba! Father!', so all true worship should have this communication between Spirit and spirit, so that we worship the Father in spirit as well as in truth. Not spirit alone, for that could be purely emotional; nor truth alone, for that could be purely intellectual. But 'all that is within me' should bless his holy name!

They were a witnessing fellowship

'Grant to thy servants to speak thy word with all boldness'—that was their great concern. And in spite of opposition, threats and beatings, 'they did not cease teaching and preaching Jesus as the Christ'. This was why the Holy Spirit had been given to them: not for great spiritual experiences, nor for lengthy discussions about the finer points of theological doctrines; but that they might be witnesses to Jesus. And providing they went everywhere preaching the word and testifying to their Saviour, the power of the Spirit went with them.

When a church or fellowship concentrates on its great commission, evangelism, that is the best and healthiest way of minimising some of the other problems that so easily arise. Whatever group we belong to, there will always be differences of opinion on secondary issues. But some words of Richard Baxter, written three hundred years ago, are highly relevant; 'The work of God must needs be done; souls must not perish while you mind your worldly business, or observe the tide and the times and take your ease, or quarrel with your brethren!' We are all on urgent business for the Master. We must therefore sink our differences, remember the fact of our oneness in Christ, and unite together to proclaim our Lord and Saviour.

CHAPTER 5

'THE GREATEST IS LOVE'

In the previous chapters of this book we have touched on some of the controversial aspects of the Spirit's work. Not all will agree with my understanding of certain issues or my interpretation of certain texts. No doubt there will always be a debate, vigorous or otherwise, concerning some of these themes. 'For now we see in a mirror dimly ... Now I know in part ...' Since on this side of heaven we shall never be united on every detail within the whole counsel of God, the one outstanding spiritual need we all have as Christians is love.

Love, more than anything else, is the hallmark of the Spirit's presence. The fruit of the Spirit is love. The love of God is poured into our hearts by the Holy Spirit. The coming of the Spirit at Pentecost meant that the apostles were enveloped by the love of God, and later it was this love that was their compelling, motivating power: 'for the love of Christ controls us', said Paul. It is interesting to note that on five occasions in Acts we read that the Spirit 'fell' on a group of people; and in four other passages in the New Testament that same word 'fell' is used in the context of an affectionate embrace. For example, the father of the prodigal son 'fell on his neck' (A.V.), or 'embraced him' (R.S.V.), when the wayward boy returned home.

Without attempting to build a doctrine on this, it is at least suggestive that the 'falling' of the Holy Spirit on someone is like a divine embrace! That is why our spirit leaps within us and cries 'Abba! Father!' We have experienced within our hearts the amazing love of God. This is the surest sign of the Spirit's activity: not only a personal experience of the love of God, but a love *for* him in return, a deep personal love relationship with Jesus Christ. 'This radiant love for Christ,' wrote A. W. Tozer, 'is to my mind the true test of catholicity, the one sure proof of membership in the church universal.'

I have a great friend who is a doctor on the mission field, and he married a fine Christian girl. For some time after their wedding they longed for a child, but none came. Then, eventually, the woman conceived and they looked forward to the tremendous event. A child was born to them, a perfectly formed child, all the fingers were there, the toes, the eyes and ears—everything was there; but it was dead. It was a very great tragedy for them. They had waited for so long, but there was no life in it at all! Sometimes that can be a picture of the body of Christ in a church. It can be all there, perfectly formed, knowing the right things, believing the right things, doing the right things—but no life, and therefore dead and without the Spirit of God.

In this concluding chapter, therefore, I want to look carefully at the greatest thing in the world, and at what is probably the most famous passage in the whole Bible, 1 Corinthians 13.

Love is more important than anything else in the sight of God, and Paul makes this clear in the opening verses.

Love is more important than speaking in tongues

Maybe I have been given by God a gift of another language, taught by the Spirit. Maybe I use it rightly as a 'love-language' by which I praise and worship the Father. No doubt I am edified by this free and spontaneous communication between my spirit and God's Spirit. I see this as a beautiful gift which refreshes my innermost being in the presence of the Lord. But, as Paul states quite clearly, 'If I speak in the tongues of men and of angels, but have not love, I am a noisy gong or a clanging cymbal.'

Love is more important than Christian maturity

I may have the gift of prophecy; I may be able to encourage and strengthen others; I may have a very deep understanding of God's word; I may be well trained and taught in the doctrines of the Christian faith; I may have the Holy Spirit revealing to me many fascinating truths out of God's word; I may have the faith to remove mountains; the faith which expects God to do mighty things, which prays for mighty things and sees God powerfully at work. That is wonderful! But Paul says in verse 2, 'If I have prophetic powers, and understand all mysteries and all knowledge, and if I have all faith, so as to remove mountains, but have not love, I am nothing.'

Love is more important than personal sacrifice
I may give money gladly and generously to God's work all over the world; I may work for Jesus every waking moment of the day; I may be so willing to sacrifice my life for him that one day I am even martyred for my faith in Christ. Yet Paul says in verse 3, 'If I give away all I have, and if I deliver my body to be burned, but have not love, I gain nothing.'

How important love is! I may have wonderful spiritual experiences; I may be wise and mature as a Christian, active, energetic, generous to a fault; and yet be nothing. The great question we need to ask ourselves is, 'Do others, when they meet with us, encounter Christ and Christ's love, or do they just meet with us?' Is it Christ or the Christian who is seen and glorified? Because without love we are nothing. It is the greatest thing in the world.

THE NATURE OF LOVE

The first half of verse 4 explains the general character of love; and then you get three sections in the remaining three verses. Here we see love overcoming problems within myself; we see love overcoming problems in my relationship with other people; and love overcoming problems in my relationship with God.

The general picture
'Love is patient', or inexhaustible. It never runs out; it never gives up. It is like the love of the father waiting patiently for his rebellious son: never turning his back on him, but waiting and hoping. What a need there is for patience within any Christian fellowship,

quite apart from the obvious needs at home or at work. We all do stupid and foolish things at times. In God's eyes we must so often speak and act as little children, fighting and squabbling over matters that seem so important to us, while forgetting the very things that are so important to God. How easily we feel hurt or resentful or irritable! How frustrated we get as we encounter the faults and failings of others! But love is patient. It goes on and on loving. It never runs out.

Then, 'love is kind', or 'it looks for a way of being constructive' (J. B. Phillips's translation). It does not mind if it is rejected or misunderstood. Always it looks positively for ways in which it can help. It is very thoughtful. Some Christians I know are always one step ahead. They anticipate some need that a person might have in the future, and they act in advance of that need. So much speaking and acting today is destructive. It is so easy to criticise and destroy. But love is not like that. It is constructive, thoughtful, helpful, kind.

Love overcomes problems within myself

In this first section, Paul mentions five such problems that rise up within us and hinder God's working in our lives.

The first is *jealousy*. We have already seen in this book something of the narrow, party spirit in the Church at Corinth. Christians belonged to several different groups, and within those groups they were clinging fiercely to their own ideas, their own ways of working, their own opinions and interpretations. They were jealously guarding what they believed was right, and arguing freely with those who disagreed with them. Let me stress that these were not disputes about the major truths of the gospel, but apparently about minor issues, doctrinal, practical and moral.[1] Of course, this jealousy in Christian circles may sometimes have a spiritual disguise. We are so anxious not to let God down! We are so concerned about defending God's truth! Does God really need our support and defence, especially in the way we are tempted to give it? But love is not jealous in another sense: it does not mind when someone else has the limelight and popularity; it is not jealous when another person is given the responsibility and privilege.

The second problem is *boasting*. Love is not boastful, or is not 'anxious to impress' (J. B. Phillips). It does not talk about its own achievements and successes. In fact love will not readily talk about itself at all; it is far more concerned with other people. And, in the context of this passage, love will not talk too readily about spiritual experiences, unless they are genuinely helpful and edifying for the body of Christ. Those at Corinth talked perhaps a little too readily about tongues, prophecies, dreams, visions and healings. Certainly there can be a time and place for sharing personal experiences, and they can be very encouraging. But Paul himself was guarded about this. Read 2 Corinthians 10–12. Even when he is forced into 'boasting' about visions and revelations, he speaks in a muted tone about some unusual experience fourteen years before when 'he heard things that cannot be told, which man may not utter'. But, Paul continues, 'I refrain from [boasting] so that no one may think more

[1] We conclude this from Acts 18: 24–19: 6; 1 Corinthians 1: 12f.; 3: 5–9 *et al.*

of me than he sees in me, or hears from me!' Love is not anxious to impress. It is much more taken up with the Lord himself and with other people.

The third problem is *arrogance*. Again J. B. Phillips has an excellent paraphrase: love does not 'cherish inflated ideas of its own importance'. The root word in the Greek is *phu*, which is onomatopoeic. It is like the sound of blowing a trumpet, or blowing up a balloon. One of the commonest snares in Christian circles is exaggeration. We talk in glowing terms about the numbers at a meeting, or about the results of a mission, or about some blessings received. At the heart of the problem is a dissatisfaction either with God or with ourselves, or with both. The facts seem too small, so we blow them up, we inflate them! In so doing, of course, we are cherishing inflated ideas of our own importance, and God has often a humbling but effective way of bursting the bubble of our pride. Love is satisfied with God, and satisfied with God's way of working (which may be to humble us!), whether the outward results are impressive or not.

The fourth problem is *rudeness*. Love is not rude. The word in the Greek is a strong word, meaning disgraceful, shameless, indecent. It is sometimes found in the context of sex. This would certainly have had special relevance at Corinth. It seems that the women there were careless about their dress; and relationships, even within the church fellowship, were far too free and easy, sometimes resulting in open immorality.[2] In the light of present-day standards, or the lack of them, Christians should be especially careful when it comes to personal behaviour. A simple test is this: If

[2] See 1 Corinthians 5–6 and 10, for example.

Christ were here with us in bodily form, would we dress like that, or behave like that? Love is not shameless, indecent or rude.

The last personal problem is *selfishness*. 'Love does not insist on its own way.' The selfish people are usually the insecure people. They are afraid of not getting their own way, or of going out to others and then getting hurt. But truly loving people are secure in that love. They accept themselves for what they are. They accept their situation, their gifts, their weaknesses and shortcomings. They are not always wishing or pretending they were someone else. They are not always thinking about themselves, or wanting more for themselves. They are content. When Jesus said, 'You must love your neighbour as yourself,' he knew exactly what he was saying. You cannot really love your neighbour until you love yourself and accept yourself as you are. It is only when you forget about your inadequacies and stop insisting on your own way, that you can go out freely in love to someone else.

Love overcomes problems in my relationship with others

Here Paul mentions four very important aspects of love.

In the first place *love is not irritable*, it is not touchy. A member of my congregation has often said this, 'If somebody rubs me up the wrong way, then I'm at fault; I should not have a wrong way to be rubbed up!' It is perfectly true. The question that is often asked is, how can we deal with somebody who gets on our nerves? The question more often should be, 'How can I deal with *myself*, if somebody gets on my nerves?' One man was irritated beyond measure by somebody that he had to work with, and he found her very difficult indeed. Because he was a Christian he was artificially polite, and he tried hard to be gracious, but in no sense was there love in his heart. So one day he prayed like this, 'Lord, I can't stand this woman. If you want her to receive love from me, then you will have to do it through me.' The record is that from that moment on, as he really prayed that prayer, he was given such a love for this woman that she herself changed, and everyone wondered what had happened, not to him, but to her. She responded to that love and she herself changed. You see, what irritates me in the life of another person is often caused by a lack of love in me towards that person. Dr. Griffith Evans of the Medical Research Council in England conducted experiments for twenty-five years with honeymoon couples, and injected the honeymoon couples with a virus of the common cold. But never once, throughout the twenty-five years of these experiments, did a honeymoon couple catch a cold! He came to the conclusion that, if there is real love and joy in the system, then this will protect the person against disease.[2] It will also protect us from the disease of an irritable, critical spirit, and so bring a measure of healing to those who upset us.

Next, *love is not resentful*, or it does not keep account of evil. The wonder of God's love is that he not only forgives us all our sins, but he forgets about them. He puts our sins behind his back; he casts them into the depths of the sea; as far as the east is from the

<hr>

[2] Quoted by Anne White in *Healing Adventure*, Arthur James, p. 55.

west, so far he removes our transgressions from us. These are some of the great promises of God in the Bible. He remembers our sins and our misdeeds no more. Real love will always both forgive and forget. Yet one of the greatest and commonest problems in the lives of people today is this matter of bitterness and resentment. Many people feel that they have been so hurt that they cannot possibly forgive; or at least they can never forget. However, true forgiveness means that we are willing to dismiss the matter altogether. Henry Ward Beecher once said that 'every man should have a fair-sized cemetery in which to bury the faults of his friends'. It is so easy keeping lists of people's faults, storing in our memory the times and ways in which we have been hurt. Such memories will always plague and disturb, they poison our whole life. Some people are physically, mentally and spiritually crippled by resentment. All those damaging lists need therefore to be burnt in the fire of God's love. Where there is a deep and serious problem, it can even be helpful writing down on a piece of paper all our 'hurts'—both ways in which we have been hurt, and ways in which we have hurt other people. Then bring this list to God in prayer; surrender the first half to him, and ask forgiveness for the other half. After that, burn the piece of paper, as a helpful sign that God both forgives and forgets, and that he wants us to do the same.

Next, *love does not rejoice at wrong*. It does not gloat over the wickedness of other people. We are often tempted to do this because, if we think about other people's mistakes, then we ourselves stand out in better light. Therefore in self-defence we are often suspicious or critical of other people, almost waiting for them to make their mistakes and behave in a certain way. 'There you are! I told you so! I knew they would do it sooner or later. I knew they would fail!' Then we feel a nasty smug feeling that we are superior, we are one up, we are not so bad as some, at least not so bad as that person down the road. Well, love does not gloat over the weakness of other people. It is sad and concerned and prayerful when it sees things which are wrong.

Lastly, in this section, *love rejoices in the right*, or delights in the truth. In other words, it is positive, it sees the best in people. I will never forget one particular person who was with me in theological college. He was shortly after his Ordination killed in a car crash, but I remember him very vividly indeed. I was all too often grumbling and grousing about this and that; but I never heard one unpleasant word said by him about anyone at any time. Whenever I complained about somebody he would at once say, 'Ah, yes, but you don't understand: his father is very ill' or something like that. Always making excuses, always trying to find something that was right. And because of that, everybody loved him.

Love overcomes problems in my relationship with God

I am thinking now, not of problems due to sin (sin will always cause problems), but problems caused because I do not always understand what God is doing or why he is doing it. Therefore, *love bears all things*, or, love knows no limit to its endurance. And the word 'bear' means 'throw a cloak of silence over what is displeasing to me'. In other words, if things are tough and difficult and I do not understand what is happening, instead of rebelling and saying 'Why, why is God doing this?' I bear it silently in love. I throw a cloak of silence over what is displeasing, over what I cannot understand. I bear it patiently because I believe that God knows what he is doing. 'Not my will but thine be done.'

Next, *love believes all things*, or has no end to its trust. At times we may feel as though God has withdrawn himself from us. We do not feel his presence or his reality at all. We feel abandoned by him, left in the darkness, lost. There may be many reasons for this, of course, but sometimes he will be testing our faith and love. We need to learn that 'even the darkness is not dark to thee, the night is as bright as the day; for darkness is as light with thee' (Psalm 139: 12). In particular we need to learn this when prayer seems to be unanswered. We claim God's promise, and nothing seems to happen; we pray for a friend who is sick, and they die. Love, however, goes on believing in spite of the darkness.

Again, *love hopes all things*. This is an extension of the last thought. It is the confident hope of Paul that we find in 2 Corinthians 4, when he says, in a passage about suffering, 'So we do not lose heart. Though our outer nature is wasting away, our inner nature is being renewed every day. For this slight momentary affliction is preparing for us an eternal weight of glory beyond all comparison' (verse 16f.; cf. Romans 8: 18–39).

How could he write such things? Because he knew the love of God in his heart.

Love endures all things

Paul once prayed for Ephesian Christians that they might be 'rooted and grounded in love'. He knew well enough that if the roots of their Christian faith could be deeply bedded into love, then they would not be shaken, even by the very worst of storms. Love continues to rejoice in a God of love, in every testing situation. That, of course, is one of the most priceless and profound lessons that we can ever learn. 'Rejoice in the Lord always,' wrote Paul to a group of Christians who were not always in harmony with one another. He goes on later to explain the value of this: 'For I have learned, in whatever state I am, to be content. I know how to be abased, and I know how to abound; in any and all circumstances I have learned the secret of facing plenty and hunger, abundance and want. I can do all things in him who strengthens me' (Philippians 4: 4, 11–13). No wonder that love is the greatest thing in the world!

One final question: How can I know this quality of love in my own life? Seeing that this is so important and yet so challenging, how can it become more true in my own experience? What we must never forget is that this is a supernatural love, a quality of love only to be found in God himself. All the struggling and striving in the world will not produce this love in our hearts. Each day, therefore, we need to come to God conscious of our personal need. We must confess our lack of love, our coldness towards him, our criticisms about others—any denial of love which exists in our hearts. Then we need to trust that God will fill our emptiness, according to his promise. 'God's love has been poured into our hearts through the Holy Spirit which has been given to us' (Romans 5 : 5). If we come daily to be filled afresh with the Spirit of God, then inevitably the fruit of love will increasingly be evident in our lives. God will give us the greatest thing in the world, which will revolutionalise not only our own lives but also the lives of those around us. Whatever other interest we may have concerning the person and work of the Holy Spirit of God, may this be our consuming ambition: *'Make love your aim.'* That is the only way in which we shall truly become one in the Spirit.